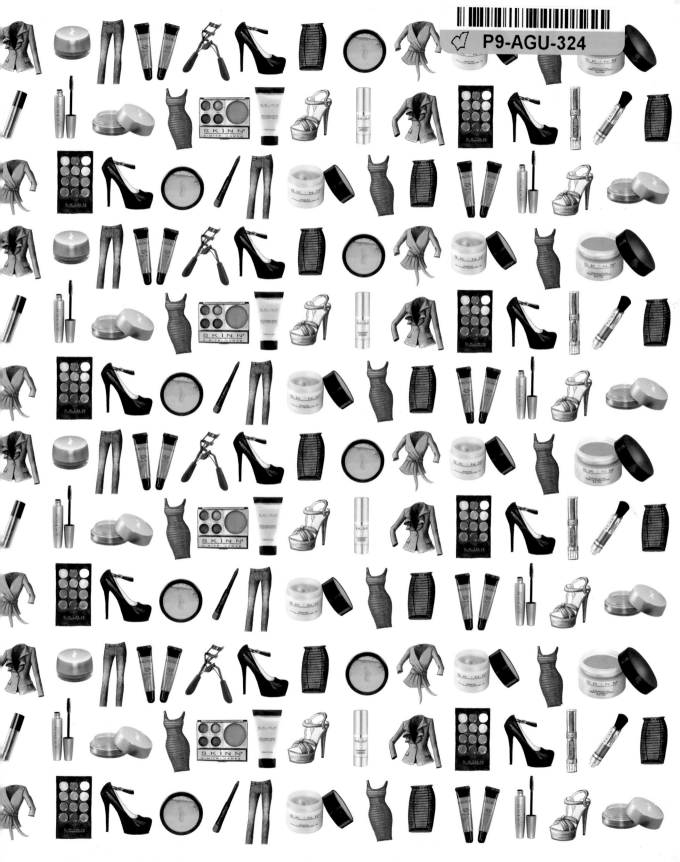

www.skinn.com

Naughty Makeovers ♥ FOR Nice Girls

HOW TO TURN UP THE **HEAT** AND ADD **SEX APPEAL** TO EVERYDAY SITUATIONS

BY DIMITRI JAMES

WITH JEAN PENN

ILLUSTRATIONS BY MEGHANN POWELL

HOW TO TURN UP THE **HEAT** AND ADD **SEX APPEAL** TO EVERYDAY SITUATIONS

DIMITRI JAMES

COPYRIGHT © 2011 DIMITRI JAMES
SKINN COSMETICS, INC.
PUBLISHED BY SKINN COSMETICS, INC.
4733 TORRANCE BLVD. STE. 974
TORRANCE, CA 90503
WWW.SKINN.COM

ISBN 978-1-4507-8385-952400

FIRST EDITION, 2011

WRITTEN BY DIMITRI JAMES WITH JEAN PENN
TEXT COPYRIGHT © BY DIMITRI JAMES
ILLUSTRATION COPYRIGHT © BY MEGHANN POWELL
ART DIRECTION AND BOOK DESIGN: MIKA KYPRIANIDES
COPY EDITING: ARLINE INGE

PRINTED AND BOUND IN THE UNITED STATES OF AMERICA
BY PRESTON LITHO + STUDIO

Acknowledgments

Ever since my business partner Joe Peri and I launched SKINN Cosmetics in 2002, the customers who came back to us again and again for more products, telling us exactly what they need, have been our inspiration and guiding light. Thank you, repeat customers. Your loyalty has ignited the growth of SKINN Cosmetics in Europe, Australia, Canada and the United States. Without your support and contact, our journeys would not have been any fun. And this book would never be.

DIMITRI JAMES

His magical ability to see and bring out the beauty in everyone is what makes Dimitri James, the creator of SKINN Cosmetics, a supreme makeover artist.

His mother and both grandmothers were European-trained aestheticians. From an early age he watched them make their own soaps, toners and masks at home, using pure, natural ingredients, and says he was always intrigued by the beauty and skin care process. Not surprisingly, he went on to become a licensed aesthetician and served as a makeup artist for beauty brands such as Estée Lauder, Chanel, Revlon, Lancôme and Borghese. In addition, he has trained makeup artists and aestheticians for Adrien Arpel Salons and Spas.

"I learned the money spent by cosmetic companies does not always go into the product. With SKINN Cosmetics, it does." His line of treatment, color and makeup products was launched in 2002 and combines the most advanced technology and delivery systems available with time honored beauty traditions. SKINN treatment and color cosmetic products are full of highly active, concentrated natural ingredients and devoid of the excess water and fillers used in most cosmetics. They are pure and effective, without sulfates or petrochemicals and other unwanted and unnecessary ingredients. Every product in the line, including makeup, also has treatment benefits. **SKINN is good for your skin.** The mineral makeup, for instance, uses cotton instead of talc. So, instead of fancy packaging, you get the most effective product, manufactured on-site at the company's Southern California headquarters, under Dimitri's highly trained and watchful eye.

SKINN is a top selling international brand on ShopNBC (U.S.), The Shopping Channel (Canada) and TVSN (Australia).

Dimitri's first book, *Becoming Beauty*, his high energy, informative makeovers and demos on television have earned him a built-in audience and legions of loyal fans across the globe.

Dimitri's work and products are frequently featured on the runway and red carpet events in New York and Los Angeles, as well as on television, in music videos and in fashion magazine spreads.

The Naughty mantra....
....Repeat after me:

Sexiness does not just belong to
the beautiful, young, thin and adorable.

Naughty knows no size.

It doesn't matter what shape I am in,
how old or how much time
and money I have to spend on myself.
I can still be sexy, fun, flirtatious and
pulled together with clothes and makeup
customized to accentuate my positives
and distract from my negatives.

Contents

Introduction

The inspiration for this book came from my frustration in dealing with Jill, who never listens to me. My young friend always plays it safe with clothes, hair and makeup, and, as a result, never gets noticed. Even though she's smart, savvy and works hard, she is taken for granted at the office. She meets plenty of men, but they rarely ask her out. When she does date, usually via the Internet, she spends the evening trying to sell herself as Good Wife material. She is so bound by all the Nice Girl rules, so afraid to stand out or appear "trashy" that she never takes chances and refuses to heat up her look with a little sex appeal. The woman is terrified of disapproval. Sound familiar?

"Nice Girls finish last. Show a little naughty once in a while," I tell her when she bitches about being lonely and overlooked at work. "You have everything going for you," I say, "You have good features, flawless skin and a cute, trim figure, and you are smart and have a good job. You are what men want. You're just not packaging yourself in the best way to get their attention."

Recently, Jill had a birthday party for herself, and I went early to help out.

She wore flattering black wide-legged slacks with a cute ruffled halter top that displayed her great tanned shoulders and back. "Yes. Yes. You look terrific. But your legs would look longer in heels." She, as usual, was wearing her precious Tory Burch flats. "These are more comfortable," she said, and wrinkled up her nose as if comfort was excuse enough on a special evening when the spotlight would be on her. I know she is afraid of being taller than a lot of men, so I pressed my lips together and spoke no more. Then, just as the first guests rang the door bell, she put on a cardigan sweater, which she wore the rest of the evening.

"For goodness sake, take the sweater off," I hissed when we brought in the birthday cake, and I got out my camera for a Kodak moment.

"I don't want to get chilly."

I groaned and rolled my eyes but took the picture, which she planned to upload to her computer for another of her online dating ventures. You would think she would want to draw attention to her good points, at least while she was posing for a picture she hoped would attract men.

Jill has a cute shape, wears quality clothes, has good taste and spends plenty on her grooming and upkeep. She is so buttoned up, however, it's hard to remember what she is wearing or looks like.

She is forgettable because she doesn't know how to market herself at home or work. She is a Nice Girl who deserves the best, but she just didn't know how to

Here are eight things you can do to show a little naughty in a hurry:

1. Let down the ponytail and fluff out your hair.

2. Trade the flats for some great high heels or wedges.

3. Add a little bright gloss or lipstick to your lips and an extra healthy coat of blackest black mascara.

4. Find that one pair of perfect jeans that make you feel sexy and confident and show off your assets.

5. Throw on a shift dress, wrap-around dress, cross-over dress or top.

6. Tighten up those loose bra straps.

7. Dab on a little perfume.

8. Splurge on a great pair of shades. Besides protecting your eyes, they add mystery and attitude.

play up her assets, and she has a lot of competition.

She tries. Her ambition in life is to be a wife and mother, with the right man, hopefully upper middle class, while continuing to work in the legal field as long as she can. A nice Catholic girl from a working class background, she has the *Preppy Handbook* rules memorized.

She dresses for the part she wants to play. Her big fear is appearing cheap or not classy. Instead of choosing fashions that flatter her trim but slightly pear-shaped body and colors that play up her beautiful skin, friendly blue eyes and sweet, feminine personality, she copies the styles worn by women in the happy wife role to which she aspires. She wears her cashmere twin sets and pearls like she once wore her Catholic girl's school uniform. Her naughty school friends had the pleated kilts shortened and the blazers tailored, but not Jill. Hers was straight from the sale rack or catalogue. Of course, it was her friends who got ogled by girl-watching guys who drove by in their snappy cars or shopped in the drugstore at the corner by the school. And today, it's her same old high school friends, many of whom have had breast enhancement surgery, who get all the attention when they travel in a pack.

Recently, they all went to Las Vegas for a weekend. Before she left, I gave her some flirting tips to get male attention in a club or bar scene.

She ignored my blunt flirting advice and played her usual Good Wife role while her pals wore their trashiest, flashiest best and got all the stud action. I won't say anymore about what happened that weekend. Except that, for Jill, it was a

disaster and humiliation. When she told me all about it, she dwelled on the popularity of boob jobs among her friends and blamed her failure on her perfectly nice chest.

"I have no feeling pro or con concerning breast enhancement, as long as the boobs fit your body," I told her. "Most of your girlfriends have gone too far. And if you do it, you have to understand it's not going to change your life. Let's face it," I continued. "The world is trashing out, especially your age group. The party celebs you see all the time on television, those bigger-than-life girls who go clubbing, are your role models. It's easy for a guy to overlook the Nice Girl because there are so many fake boobs and other distractions. Because you're so nice, you just wait for guys to come up and talk to you.

"If you don't get men to stop and look, you're never going to get them to listen. You have to set the bait, get their attention. It's like the crazy colors you see at the cosmetics counter at the department store. The cosmetic business is 80 percent browns and beiges, but the industry knows that it's the hot pinks and bright blues that make you stop and look."

None of this cheered her up at all. I took another tack.

"You don't need big boobs to look sexy to men," I said. "You have other great body parts, a cute ass, terrific skin and very nice legs. You just have to show them off."

She shrugged. "The kind of man I want is looking for a clean-cut, outdoorsy, athletic looking woman."

"Men love Naughty Women," I told her. "They love Trashy Women, too, but for all the wrong reasons.

How to attract men at a club or bar:

It's like fishing.
Use the best bait,
hook him and
then reel him in.

1 Check out the room and single out the man you want. Make lots of eye contact. Try short, darting gazes at him and then look away. Next, deliver a direct gaze more than three seconds. Add a little head toss and hair flip.

2 Give the object of your attention a big smile.

3 If you are really daring, a little hello with your hand will be effective.

4 Remember, men like to see a girl laughing and having fun, not uptight.

5 Get up and dance with your girlfriends. And have fun. A little flirtatious dancing always gets men's attention, much more so than standing at the wall or bar like a wallflower. Men get turned on seeing girls dance with other girls, but sexy grinding on the dance floor with other guys will make them think you are taken.

6 Know that most men will not approach without eye signals. Of course, when a hottie sends out available signs, the penis takes over all normal thought processes. When on "penis alert," a man is blind to all the usual warning signs and is totally vulnerable.

There is a big difference
between Trashy and Naughty.

"Trashy says come and get it.

"Naughty says, 'I know you want it, but you're not hungry enough yet.'

"Naughty gives men hope, intrigues them and gives them something to work for. It's the glimpse of Naughty in you that will keep them coming."

I made fashion suggestions about spicing up her work and play look but could tell she wasn't buying.

"I'd rather be myself," she said, and blinked back her tears. "I would hate to look cheap or trashy. It's just not me."

I shut my mouth. Jill will always choose to play it safe. Anything else is too scary for her. I did her makeup once before a big date, and she looked fantastic. Afterwards, she removed most of it. I stood by and watched, steaming. "Why Jill? Why!!!"

"This guy is an outdoorsy type. He likes a natural look," she said, wiping off my artistry.

I have heard those very same words from women many times. In my younger days, I worked for different cosmetics companies doing makeovers at department stores. Sometimes the woman would have her man in tow. "My husband likes a natural look," the customer would caution me. "He doesn't like me in a lot of makeup." Meanwhile, the husband would be drooling over the foxy cosmetic counter girls whose looks are totally tricked out with makeup.

After I finished the makeover, more often than not, the husband would tell his wife, "You look fabulous. Buy everything you have on."

Naughty and Nice

Both may own the essential cashmere twin set. But Naughty sometimes wears the cardigan alone, buttoned just high enough to show a hint of lace underneath.

Both avoid underwear darker than their clothes or anything that would appear transparent at work. But Naughty knows the power of suggestion. A lace bra under a silk shirt is a turn-on known to classic Naughty Girls for decades. They also love the provocative look of lace but at work wear it over a nude lining or camisole.

Natural doesn't happen after 25. Men may think they like the natural look, but most of them don't have a clue regarding how much makeup it takes for a woman over 25 to look good. That's not to say they want the woman in their life to look like a hooker, at least not most of the time.

Frankly, I've just about given up on Jill but not on all the other Nice Girls out there who need just a little naughty to spice up their lives but are afraid of looking trashy. I'm not just talking about single women. I'm talking about happily married women, including young Moms and Cougars of every age and size who need to add a little sizzle to their lives.

Ask yourself this troublesome question: Do people remember me or do I have to be constantly reintroduced?

If you are being overlooked and forgotten, remember that sexy, polished and feminine sells on all fronts. Have a dress and makeup plan for every facet of your life and agree to never look blah and forgettable again.

The plan should be fun, flattering to your shape and image and appropriate for the occasion.

In this book I will tell you how to package yourself with style for every situation. No need to schlep to the grocery store or the gym in a baggy unflattering sweat suit, no matter your age or status.

This minimal maintenance should be good enough so you can walk out the door. If you stop at the market and bump into a guy who once rejected you, you don't have to crouch behind a stack of canned food. Repackaging yourself is not hard, even expensive or terribly time consuming. It's all a matter of organizing your clothes, makeup and beauty regime. So let's begin.

Naughty

Naughty and Trashy

Black net stockings are a tease worn with boots and a long skirt, so there is just that glimpse. But don't wear them with short skirts and heels, unless you are a cocktail waitress or pole dancer.

A well-placed tattoo that is hidden on job interviews and temporary tattoos are naughty. Tramp stamps that never hide are trashy.

Platinum blond is naughty. Blown out bleachaholic, box-color blond is trashy.

Trashy

Naughty Beginnings

Getting Started

Start by giving yourself permission to be naughty, to be the star in your own life. But remember, just because Katy Perry can dash to the store in denim cutoffs, black tights and high ankle heels doesn't mean you should. Those glitzier than thou glam girls on the red carpet are part of the marketing machine to sell fashion, makeup and jewelry. Their fur chubbies and designer minis, their hairstyles, their diamonds, everything right down to the iced Grey Goose vodka in their crystal glasses, are given to them by companies, free of charge, so they can act like living billboards to move products. Their lifestyles and looks are pure fantasy and have nothing to do with the reality that is your life.

I'm not saying that they don't ignite trends, some of which you might want to interpret for yourself when you want to look young, hot and edgy. But do so only if the trend actually fits and flatters you.

In other words, if the high platform shoes and tight jeans make your butt look sweet, go for it, but choose the time and place. Don't show up at the PTA meeting looking like Lindsey Lohan. Instead, develop your own star power.

"No one will think you are beautiful unless you do." As a child, I often heard grandma saying that to my sister, and she was right.

Some lucky girls learn from their mothers how to package and project themselves to turn heads. But if mom didn't know herself, where is a girl to turn?

Well, nice girls everywhere, regardless of what

mom did or did not tell you, I'm here to help. And I say that every woman has the right to look hot whenever or wherever she wants. You just need to learn the tricks of using fashion and makeup to your best advantage.

When you know how to look pulled together, stylish and sexy with minimal effort for all the different occasions in your life, you will feel more confident, and people will see a person worth noticing, someone who feels good about herself.

What styles and cuts flatter you?

Gwyneth Paltrow or Katie Holmes can wear a belt around a suit jacket or a long fringed scarf around their waist and not look like someone's grandma from the old country. Tall, lean, flat-tummied, narrow-hipped, long-necked creatures look great in any clothes.

If you are so blessed, enjoy. If not, remember, **looking great is all about smoke and mirrors, dressing to accentuate the good and eliminate the bad.** Pick your best body part, be it a waspy waist, a great bust or a bodacious butt, and make sure it is noticed.

If like Michelle Obama, you have toned arms and shoulders, go for sleeveless dresses and tops. If your best attribute is long, slender legs and a great ass, that sequined miniskirt might be an excellent purchase. If you have great breasts, a little décolletage goes a long way.

The body most men go for is medium weight and curvy, not super thin. The clothes the Naughty Girl favors are designed to make women look as close to that curvaceous hourglass shape as possible.

It's all smoke and mirrors:

💜 **If you are heavy**
Say yes to: Long, loose, flowing layers of tightly woven fabrics that are body skimming rather than clingy or stretchy.
Say no to: Big, bold patterns. To add color pizzazz, limit brights and patterns to oblong scarves or vests under jackets.

💜 **If you are petite**
Say yes to: Tailored clothing such as pants with tapered legs, jackets with tapered sleeves, narrow belts and shorter, slimmer skirts or even long slim skirts.
Say no to: Pleats, layers and oversized or boxy clothing, A-line skirts, plaids, polka dots and stripes.

❤ **If you are pear-shaped**
Say yes to: Scoop and boat necks, light layering, light-color wrap sweaters and blazers over bright tops. Dark, boot-cut pants.

❤ **If you have large thighs**
Say yes to: Thigh-slimming undergarments, heavy fabrics that fall straight down only as wide as necessary to skim over the thighs, dark colors, loose skirts with drapes or pleats.
Say no to: Corduroy, denim, tight skirts or stretchy pants unless covered with tops, sweaters or jackets.

❤ **If you have big boobs**
Say yes to: Fitted jackets with a deep V and hem cut to the hip, V-necks that slenderize and show off your décolletage.
Say no to: High, round necks, turtlenecks and Empire lines.

❤ **If you have a big butt**
Say yes to: Loose-fitting, wide-legged trousers with a lower waistline and a tailored jacket that nips the waist and flairs over the hips, black bottoms with bright tops, flared or pencil-shaped skirt.
Say no to: High-waisted trousers and jackets that end at the butt.

❤ **If you are short, round and full**
Say yes to: High heels, body-skimming clothing, fitted sleeves, tapered pants, simple layering, basic black, tailored tops, button earrings, jewelry that falls below the bustline, long and narrow scarves that hang past the waistline.
Say no to: Flat shoes, tight fitting clothing, loose and flowing sleeves, palazzo pants, bulky layers, belted jackets, long hair, chokers, turtlenecks, patterned hosiery, horizontal stripes, short skirts, wide belts, cropped jackets.

Get together ten outfits that fit, flatter and look fabulous.

When it comes to your closet, less is more. You probably don't need more clothes, shoes and handbags. You need better total outfits.

Once you remove the clutter, it's easy to get dressed quickly. Get rid of all the mistakes you never should have bought and start organizing your closet into pieces that go together. **If it doesn't look good on you, you don't need it cluttering up space.** All of your looks, from office to mom duty, in and out of the house and everywhere you go, should be fun and feminine, flattering and fit perfectly. All you have to do is throw everything else away.

Take some time and put together some total looks for different situations in your life. When you buy something, always know where you will wear it and, if possible, buy a total put together outfit that blends with the rest of your clothes.

The Nice Girl often follows cookie-cutter trends and fails to look special or else sees the fashion industry as an evil conspiracy. She has no style at all. She has the right pieces, but they never go together. Often something is off, like the wrong kind of shoe or the wrong mix of fabric or some cut that makes her look dumpy and frumpy.

Some women know how to play with fashion, and putting themselves together is fun. For them, **bargain hunting is a diverting, calorie-burning sport and dressing is an artistic expression.** They express their personality and perhaps even their artistic side with their style, and they stand out from the crowd. So often they end up in the fashion and beauty business and always get noticed for the great looks they put together.

For those who do not have this knack, buy a total look, head to toe, from accessories to shoes, put together by someone with that same kind of savvy.

That's what men do, and believe me, it saves time. Furthermore, you don't need a celebrity stylist like Rachel Zoe. You can get it done for free on websites such as **style.com, whowhatwear.com,** and **Refinery29.com.** Stores like **Neiman Marcus** and **Nordstrom** also help you shop the total look.

Upscale fashion retailers often have very cool professional shoppers standing by to run around the store and put together the right lines, proportions, colors and looks for you. Many boutique owners are also very knowledgeable. If you look good, they look good.

Self-confidence is the key. It is okay to push the envelope with style, but don't step too far outside your comfort zone or wear clothes that don't make you look beautiful. **Focus on playing up your strength, rather than hiding your flaws.**

Naughty fashion dos:

- ♥ Be on a first-name basis with a good alterations person.

- ♥ Look for fabrics that fall smoothly over your curves or look inviting to touch like silk, cashmere or velvet. But choose wisely with the latter. Velvet can go so wrong.

- ♥ Wear matching tops and bottoms to look taller, sleeker. One great look is pants and a matching sweater in the color of your choosing, with a jacket in a contrasting color.

- ♥ Wear bright colors near the part of the body you like.

- ♥ If you wear stripes, make sure the outfit is on the loose side.

- ♥ Wear short jackets over long or full skirts and long jackets with skinny pants, unless you want to show off a great ass in skin-tight jeans.

- ♥ A pin on the shoulder diverts attention away from a thick waist.

- ♥ Wearing the same color hem and stockings makes you look taller, thinner and disguises thick ankles.

- ♥ Bags bring attention to wherever they fall. If you have big hips, don't wear a hip length shoulder bag. If you have a full bust, don't carry a clutch under your arm. If you have a small waist, let the bag call attention to that area of the body.

If you've got a beautiful pair of legs, play that up with a skirt or nice tailored shorts that show them off. If you have a shapely behind, invest in a nice pair of jeans and have them tailored to accentuate your best asset. If you have a full chest, wear a flattering wrap-style top. If you have great arms and shoulders, wear a tank top. If you have bright eyes, choose an accessory that matches them, something that makes the color pop. Stand up straight, walk with your head high and portray yourself as the strong woman that you are. Remember that a smile (even if it's a rough day) does wonders to lift your mood. It also makes you seem more friendly and approachable.

Your best friend is a good alterations person.

Don't expect to buy tailored clothes off the rack and have them fit properly. When you shop for quality items at sales, if the smaller size is a wee tight, don't buy it and promise yourself to lose five pounds so you can wear it. Instead, **buy a size larger and take it to the alterations person.** Expect to spend some money, but it's worth it to have clothes look like they were made for you.

The Naughty Girl has many of the basics, including, most particularly, a black slim skirt, but hers was bought a wee bit too big, then perfectly tailored to fit her cute rear end with cupping.

Don't expect to buy tailored clothes off the rack and have them fit properly.

The black skirt is half of a suit and there are also pants. All are perfectly fitted. By pairing the pants with cute tops and the suit with various blouses, she transforms one suit into many looks.

She knows snug sleeves are the sexiest, has blouses taken in at the waist, if that is her strong point, and always buys one size up from the pant that shows pant lines or a crease under the butt, knowing it will look great when altered.

What's wrong with being high maintenance?

Okay, so it's human to let beauty and makeup rituals slip when life gets crazy. But I say, unless you are a woman like Hillary Clinton or Christiane Amanpour, racing against time to help solve the great problems of the world, there are no really good excuses. And remember, you would never see either of them without makeup. **Make a pact to never leave the house without the basic five-minute makeup outlined here.** You'll be surprised how much difference those five minutes can make.

Nice Girls are often so busy taking care of other people, that they forget themselves. Allow yourself some selfish time to develop other beauty habits and get started on the road to hot and sexy.

After you get your closet and makeup drawer organized, your Naughty Girl Look should not take you long to get together in the morning. At night, you need just five minutes to properly cleanse your face and put on your face serum, eye serum and night cream.

The weekly beauty regimes, spelled out here in this chapter, are simple and quick, a delicious indulgence.

Promise yourself a face scrub or mask, a body scrub or body polish once a week. You deserve it, and the benefits will be the payoff, not just about how you look, but how you feel about yourself. I recommend my DermAppeal Scrub twice a week every week.

Once you organize your arsenal and learn how to use clothes and makeup to your advantage, no matter what shape you are in or where you are going, you will look pulled together, stylish and fun. And you will feel better about yourself.

Forward march, standing tall and shoulders back.

Good posture will make a huge improvement in your appearance and attitude. When you slouch, your tummy bulges and breasts sag and you are silently broadcasting low self-esteem.

Here's what I learned at my aunt Lyn's modeling school:

Back against a wall with your chin up and your spine straight; your head, shoulder blades, heels and buttocks pushed up against the wall; then walk away without changing your position.

Practice this exercise frequently and you will soon have better posture. **When you catch yourself slouching, find the nearest wall and adjust your position.**

After a while, good posture will become second nature. **Another good posture exercise is walking while balancing a book on your head.**

The Naughty Girl closet includes:

- Lace-trimmed camisoles

- Layered tops to make legs look longer and waist look smaller

- Scoop neck and boat-necked tops in shiny or textured colors that make shoulders look wider

- Wrapped tops and V-neck T-shirts in flattering colors and black and white

- Light-layering pieces such as a T-shirt under a wrap sweater or a blazer over a bright top

- Dark straight or boot leg pants that make legs look longer

- Simple, flared, flirty and frivolous skirts

- Cap-sleeve jacket to wear over camisole

- Cardigan sweater to wear over tailored shirt

- Structured fabric blazer such as leather, denim, suede or velvet that nips in at the waist and has wider shoulders

- Waist-flattering sweaters that fit snugly and stop at the hip

- Pull-on boots, tight around the middle, to wear with longer skirts or short skirts and matching tights or even black net stockings

- A slimming deep V-neck sweater to wear over white camisole or undershirt

- A well-pressed blouse with long sleeves, one size larger than the size with buttons popping

- A well-fitted blouse, especially around the waist and bust

- Well-fitted jacket and pants just one size up from the one that shows panty lines or a crease under the butt

- Shoes and socks color coordinated to pants or skirts for longer, leaner look

- Capri pants as long as they are black slim cut, a la Audrey Hepburn and no more than three to four inches above the middle of the ankle

- Pedal pushers no

Your getting started beauty plan

Every day, if you drink 8 glasses of water, get 6 to 8 hours' sleep and 30 minutes of aerobic exercise, avoid sun exposure, cleanse your face in the morning and apply at a minimum the 5-minute light makeup outlined here, you will feel and look better in no time. Reducing salt in your diet, especially in the evening, will also make a difference.

No, you do not have to use my products to achieve the transformation from boring to hot. It just makes it easier when you work with the best tools of the trade. You wouldn't try to cook a gourmet meal with Barbie's Easy Bake Oven utensils or prepare sushi with a butcher knife, would you? On the other hand, I don't want to scare you off. Whatever tools you may already have or are willing to buy, the point is to get into the kitchen and start cooking. Of course, I stand by my own products, but I also realize that, depending on the shape of your cosmetic and beauty drawer, you might want to go at it slowly, filling in where needed until we have made you into a total convert.

For your morning and evening cleansing routines, you will need:

- Morning cleanser
- Night cleanser (oil based)
- Good day cream
- Good night cream that agrees with your skin
- Great eye cream

Recommended products:

Sulfate Free Gentle Exfoliating Cleanser

Olive & Enzyme Rich Balm Cleanser

Collagenesis Twenty-Four Hour Youth Preservation Cream

Collagenesis Stem Rejen Eye Lifting Serum

Nice Girls love to be
all squeaky clean.

They wash vigorously with soaps and scrubs,
including glycerin soaps, to get all the dirt
away, not realizing that they are stripping
their skin of some of its natural moisture
factors and altering its ideal pH. Please be
especially wary of over-the-counter cosmetic
cleansers that bubble up.

To cleanse your face in the A.M. use
an acid-based, gentle exfoliating wash.
My **Sulfate Free Gentle Exfoliating
Cleanser** uses an active ingredient,
found in aspirin, to unplug pores and to
exfoliate and resurface the skin. You apply a
little to your damp face and neck, massage
for one moment and splash off. It does
double duty as a pore refining mask
treatment. Once or twice a week,
rub it on, wait for 5 minutes, then
come back to the sink and splash it
off. You'll be amazed how good your
skin feels afterwards.

The same goes for my **Olive &
Enzyme Rich Balm Cleanser**, that can
be rinsed off with a warm, wet washcloth,
removing your eye makeup as well as the
day's pollution from your face. This cleanser
also doubles as a mask. You can leave it on
for 5 to 10 minutes once or twice a week for
a deep cleansing, nourishing, softening and
line-smoothing treatment.

My **Collagenesis Twenty-Four
Hour Youth Preservation Cream**
serves as a day and night cream. It is the
result of the most cutting-edge technology
in anti-aging ingredients from
17 different countries.

Harsh chemical sunscreens
are not good for your skin and
should always go on over day
cream or moisturizer. You have
options. If you are outdoors a lot
and want more coverage,
go with **Skinnsurance Natural
Mineral Sunscreen SPF 30**
and apply it after face cream. To
save time, there are products that combine
foundation with sun block, such as my
**High Definition Mineral &
Cotton Powder
Foundation**
or my
**Plasma
Foundation**
with coordinating concealer.

To improve and protect the skin
around the eyes, I recommend my
**Collagenesis Stem Rejen Eye
Lifting Serum** both at night and
under your concealer.

Makeup supplies

Wearing the same makeup all the time is boring. In future chapters, I'll outline makeup instructions and tips on eyebrows, corrective eye makeup and contouring. What follows here are the basics for your five-minute minimal makeup, as well as suggested products to be used now and later. And because some skin needs more coverage, and because all Naughty Girls love options, I have included a few:

- Darkest black mascara
- Eyelash curler
- 1 black or dark brown eyeliner
- Eyeshadows selected to complement each other in a neutral shade. Choose shadows in monochromatic shades, not extreme opposites.
- Concealer, if needed and if wearing foundation. A mineral powder foundation with SPF 15 also doubles as a concealer when applied with a small brush if you need less coverage.
- A blush or bronzing powder that can also be used on the eyes and cheeks.
- 1 lipstick
- 1 gloss

Recommended Skinn products

Luxe Premier Fiber Optic Mascara

No Damage Lash Curler

Orchid Gel Mattefying Day Treatment

Twin Set Collagen Boost Lipstick & Wet Lips Gloss

High Definition Cotton & Mineral Foundation or my Plasma Foundation & Concealer

Smudge Sticks

Luxe Premier Fiber Optic Mascara conditions and fills in missing or thinning lashes with real silk fibers. It's like applying individual lashes with every coat. And while many eyelash curlers merely bend and kink, you'll find mine really curls and is easy to handle. It won the 2011 Beauty Award from *Essence* magazine.

My **High Definition Cotton & Mineral Foundation** has the sunscreen you need and **is also** the world's first mineral makeup to include laser-cut cotton in its foundation. It goes on with a brush and is great when you are in a hurry. Just apply with a smaller brush under eyes and other areas where you want extra coverage. You say a mineral foundation doesn't provide enough coverage? My **Plasma Foundation**, also with sun block, can be purchased with a matching concealer that will not crease, cake or clump.

Smudge Sticks are fat pencils that work as eyeliner and shadow. They glide on effortlessly in versatile colors. We'll be using them for many looks in future chapters.

For lipstick, I suggest my **Twin Sets Collagen Boost Lipstick & Wet Lips Gloss**, which take the mystery out of finding the perfect match between your lipstick and gloss. My favorite colors are Berry Glam and Skinny Dip.

As for eyeshadow, you have several options. For a dual-purpose product that works with our 5-minute makeup, try my

Color Touch Eye, Cheek & Lip Glow. These little pots of color that look like a cream blush can be used as eyeshadow, as well as cheek and lip color. Maybe you already own a case with three shadows in neutral shades that are selected to complement one another. The colors should be in monochromatic shades, not extreme opposites. For eyeshadows to take you through all the looks I will discuss in the book, check our **Luxe Premier Eyeshadow**. It gives you a lot of bang for your buck, with 12 complementary colors. My shadows are talc free, so even lined or crepey eyelids will look smooth.

Orchid Gel Mattefying Day Treatment, used alone or under makeup, brightens the complexion, smoothes skin, locks in moisture and offers the ideal blendable camouflage for flaws. Its light lavender color neutralizes yellow undertones and evens out consistency and coloration. If used alone, apply it over **Skinnsurance Natural Mineral Sunscreen SPF 30.**

Five-minute minimal makeup
Never leave the house without it:

1. Use eyedrops.

2. Moisturize your face with a day cream.

3. Apply Orchid Gel Mattefying Day Treatment either alone or under a foundation with sun block protection.

4. Dot concealer around brow bone, lid and under the eye to conceal circles and blend well. Option: Apply mineral powder foundation with smaller brush under eyes and areas that need more cover.

5. Pull eyelid taut with your middle finger at the outer corner near the hairline and apply Smudge Stick in Venus or Egyptian Clay or your eyeliner of choice to the lash line, drawing a thin line from the outside corner inward. Blend with brush.

6. Instead of using eye-shadow, sweep bronzer, blush or my Color Touch Eye, Cheek & Lip Glow over the entire eyelid up to the brow.

7. Apply black mascara to the upper and/or lower lashes.

8. Line lips fat and thick with Smudge Stick and apply favorite lip gloss. Option: Apply your favorite Twin Set Collagen Boost Lipstick & Wet Lips Gloss.

You are out the door...

What's that? You have 90 more seconds to spare in front of the mirror? Add a little eyeshadow instead of bronzer. Choose a darker shade of smoky matte shadow and a complementary lighter shade in the same hue. Using an angled liner or brow brush, apply darker shade over entire eyelid. Use lighter highlighting shade under brow bone.

Choose
lipstick shades
to show off
your eyes.

Select matte or
cream formulations
of lipstick in the
following shades:

Blue eyes
Rose, pink, bronze,
copper, brown, dark
claret red

Hazel eyes
Violet, plum, fuchsia,
red-violet

Green eyes
Mauve, lavender,
plum, burgundy,
wine

Brown eyes
Coral, peach,
burgundy, purple,
gold-red, nude-
beige and dark
blue-red

Hair makes or breaks your total look.

Choose a style that respects the integrity of your hair. If you have curly hair, find a style that does not need to be worn straight in order to look good and vice versa. The first place to splurge is on a good hair stylist, not only for cuts but also color. It is money well spent to achieve a cut and color that is good for your type of hair and flattering to your face. If you color your hair, match your natural shade as closely as possible to make regrowth more graceful and save on constant touch-ups. Avoid chunky or heavily highlighted hair unless you have the resources to maintain it often.

A shade darker brightens lighter skin tones. A shade lighter brightens darker skin tones. You can divert attention away from any prominent features of your face that you don't like by creating fullness in your hair. Soft highlights also help draw the eye away from the face and to the hair. Big hair does date you, but men love long hair. That's why extensions are naughty.

About hair color and skin

A good hair colorist understands the relationship of hair color and skin tones. For instance: **For ruddy pink or reddish skin,** say no to red-gold or strawberry blond. Go for ash with blue and violet undertones.

For golden, sallow or yellow-olive undertones, say no to colors with golden, amber, yellow or orange undertones. Go for shades of natural blond, brown or deep burgundy red.

If your skin is light, a rich dark red shade will make it look like porcelain.

For olive skin, avoid anything too light. If you must go blond, first bleach out all the color in your hair, and then add shade of blond back in with a low peroxide color or toner.

Women of color should stay as close to natural as possible. For a fantasy color look, choose a color that is the opposite of your skin tone, i.e., for golden or yellow-brown skin, go with blue undertones, such as burgundy or wine instead of orange or golden-red. The same holds for going blond. Choose ash-blue or bright blonds instead of yellow or golden.

To hide damaged hair, go a shade or two darker.

For thin hair, consider reverse highlighting to make it look fuller.

Save time and money on shampoos.

Nice Girls are always washing their hair. Big mistake. Hair gets frayed and worn out from too much washing. If you can hold out, shampoo once a week. If you must, between washings, rinse your hair with warm water while you rub your fingers back and forth. Pretend there is shampoo. Then rinse with cold water for extra shine. When you do shampoo, use lots of warm (not hot) water to get the hair really wet. Spend 3 to 5 minutes washing away the shampoo and rinse with cool water. Apple cider vinegar and distilled water, 50/50, really makes hair shine. Blot hair thoroughly and let it dry at least 90 percent before straightening or curling. When blow-drying your hair, use a metal core brush. It flattens the cuticles and really makes your hair shine.

Your colors:

♥ **Darker hair, lighter skin:** Cool whites, black, cool gray, navy, pale blue, true blue, royal blue, turquoise, cool aqua, emerald green, icy green

♥ **Dark hair and darker skin:** Natural white, cream, bronze, pewter, true red, scarlet, orange, true yellow, gold, royal blue, green, turquoise, pale blue, true green, emerald, pale pale pink, cerise, orchid or magenta

♥ **Light hair plus pink or ruddy skin:** Soft white, camel, rose-beige, blue-gray, warm gray, navy, pastel green, fern green, pastel pink, deep rose, cool pink, raspberry, burgundy, maroon, plum, mauve, orchid, lavender or blue violet. Avoid light shades of pink that are too similar to your skin color.

♥ **Light hair plus creamy, yellow or sallow skin:** Ivory, cream, beige, caramel, camel, warm gray, golden brown, tan, light navy, royal blue, periwinkle blue, peachy-pink, apricot, coral, rust, golden yellow or violet

♥ **Red hair and light to medium skin:** Oyster white, camel, golden beige, dark brown, tan, coffee, bronze, gold, deep blue, turquoise, earth greens, jade, dark forest green, yellow-green, peach, orange, salmon, rust, terracotta, tomato red, orange-red or brick

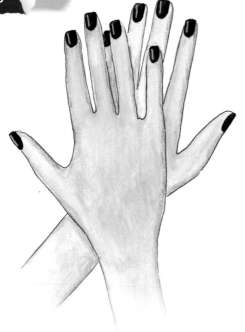

Hands up

Nails all one length and not too long, cuticles that are well kept and fresh polish, say, "I take care of myself." Whether you bother with manicures or not, keep your nails the same length and never wear them very long. If one nail breaks, cut all your nails down and start over. I think nails longer than ½-inch past the finger tips are in Porn Star territory. Shorter is better.

Short nails with dark current trend colors like black, gun metal or gray-beige are naughty. Long fake square acrylics with designs, glitter, and rhinestones are trashy.

If you are not good at keeping your nails up, a French manicure gives you the most mileage. But practical and as nice as

they may be, nails in a classic sheer beige and French nails are not very naughty.

Of course, these days nails are a controversial subject, and almost everyone has a different opinion.

"Acrylics that look like paddles make me want to puke, especially the long fake French manicure acrylics with the fake white tip." Lauren, my young, hip friend, wiggled her Argon Green fingertips to make her point. I agree, to a point. Fake nails make you look older.

Nail gels are the newest advance, and my female friends swear by them. The gel goes on like polish over the natural nail and stays for two to three weeks with never a chip until it is soaked off.

Speaking of hands, if you have large or crooked knuckles, choose large rings that detract from and/or cover the problem. Do not wear small delicate rings.

What every Miss America knows

Women are not born knowing how to walk, stand and pose with grace on a runway, be well spoken, impress the judges in interviews and talent displays and win beauty contests. That's where someone like my friend Mickey Feigelson of Birmingham and Palm Springs comes in. An approved Miss Alabama judge for the Miss America Pageant system, he consults with and coaches high school and college-age pageant contestants for Miss Alabama, Miss Teen USA, Junior Miss and Miss America titles. What are some of the things these contestants learn?

♥ You only have one chance to make a great first impression. This is true whether you are meeting a contest judge or someone at a bar.

♥ You are judged first by your overall appearance: how well you look and take care of yourself. Proper skin care helps. Good posture and carriage are much more important than you might think.

♥ Intelligence and knowledge are of equal importance to beauty. It shows in your face as well as your conversation.

♥ Foundation, powder, blush, concealer and mascara can be your best friends.

♥ The swimsuit should cover your butt, not be in it. Contestants apply a sticky spray on the seams at the bottom of a swimsuit so it will stick to the skin and not ride up while they are walking.

♥ Beauty contests can get you where you want to go. Deidre Downs Gunn, who was Miss Alabama and Miss America, competed in contests for five years. Winnings helped pay her way through med school at the University of Alabama at Birmingham. She is now an M.D.

> Don't underestimate the power that scent has to trigger precious memories and render you unforgettable.

Fragrance

Jill uses scent, but doesn't want to overpower. So taking the advice of many women's magazines, she sprays it in the air and walks through it. What a waste of expensive perfume. The Naughty Girls put on enough scent for men to say, "Mmm, what are you wearing?" when they saunter by. That's not to say you can't smell them across the room.

Somewhere between spraying it in the air and bathing in it like a whore is the Naughty Girl ideal. Whatever your scent, don't forget to dab some on your pulse, wrists, back of the knees.

Don't underestimate the power that scent has to trigger precious memories and render you unforgettable.

My **LOVE**, **LIVE** and **LAUGH** fragrances are perfume strength and come in compact roll-on bottles that are easily tucked into your handbag. We use proven scents that are linked to those very emotions. **LOVE**, for instance, features night-blooming flowers, exotic tropicals and rare spices that last for hours. The fragrances were custom blended by a professional perfumer to capture these feelings.

> Hosiery is another place to save money and drawer space.

Sheer hose is out of style and old. Never mind what Kate Middleton wears. One day she may be queen, and she comes from a cold country with lots of rules for royalty. **All the Naughty Girl really requires these days are clean-shaven toned legs with a great tan and lots of lotion on so that they look satiny and naughty.** Pull-on socks to coordinate with your pants and one pair each of black opaque and black net stockings are all else that is necessary.

Final note

This book comes with a warning label: Know there are times Nice is better than Naughty.

As I will be saying again and again, this book is about how to use clothes and makeup to market yourself for any situation. But common sense will tell you that all the world's a stage and there are situations when looking too foxy can go against you.

For instance, in his fascinating book, *Looks, Why They Matter More Than You Ever Imagined*, Gordon L. Patzer, PhD, describes the torrid trial of Ruth Snyder accused, with her lover, of murdering her husband in 1928. The jury might have spared her the electric chair, but she came to the witness stand in sheer black stockings and showed off her long legs and shapely figure with tightly tailored suits and blouses. She was a classic Naughty Girl, from her immaculate coiffure to her perfect lacquered nails. Patzer says the all-male jury figured she was a femme fatale who could easily wrap any man around her little finger, so she was executed at Sing Sing.

Famous people from Hollywood and beyond attended the trial that became the basis of James Cain's book, *Double Indemnity*, later adapted for the screen by Raymond Chandler and Billy Wilder into the classic film with Barbara Stanwyck and Fred MacMurray. Barbara Stanwyck epitomizes the Naughty Girl. One night, Nice Girls everywhere, when you are bored, rent some of her old films and take notes.

Naughty at Work

Am I actually encouraging you to look spicy and haute at work?

Yes. Yes. Yes.

I see Nice Girls get passed over again and again at work in favor of girls that are hot and pretty and have it together. This is true, even if their boss is a woman.

That's because blending into the background isn't going to make you stand out from the competition. Male or female, when you make them stop and look, they also listen.

I see the examples all around me from all the trade shows I go to, where every company puts its best-looking employees forward, to my many friends, male and female, who work for pharmaceutical companies and are flat out told to look sexy.

The talents and skills and work attitude needed to succeed are up to you. **But I can show you how to look professional and pulled together at the office so you will be sure to get the recognition that you deserve.**

Nice Girls, like my friend Jill, follow the rules, work overtime and wait politely for a promotion or a raise or more challenging assignments. They are boring in their dress, veering away from sexuality in favor of what they believe to be the Uniform for Success approach. Naughty Girls make up their own fashion rules. And they aren't afraid to appear ballsy and say, "Show me the money."

If imitation is the sincerest form of flattery, dressing like the people one level up from you is an obvious way to kiss up. That's what ambitious Nice Girls everywhere believe; never mind if the clothes their boss wears make them look dowdy and old.

For the Naughty Girls I know, dressing outside the box and turning heads is preferable to kissing up.

They enjoy flirting with fashion, standing out from the crowd and looking hot. Instead of dressing like the boss, they choose styles that flatter their shapes. They aren't the least bit afraid to make mistakes. **They would probably rather splurge on clothes and makeup than just about anything, including lunch.**

If every other woman at the office wears sweats and jeans, they choose comfortable work clothes that are occasionally flirtatious, always figure-flattering and fit perfectly. Their clothes are appropriate for their job but never boring and predictable.

Both Nice and Naughty Career Girls own identical fashion items for the office— nice sweater sets, skirts or pants with matching or contrasting blazers and good handbags.

However, the Naughty Girls I see are in short, fitted jackets and blazers in bright colors or with interesting tailoring and, on the daring end, with zippers, chains and studs. Their straight skirts are at least a little above the knee and always worn with heels. **If they have a nice tush, the skirt cups their curves gently, thanks to meticulous tailoring.** Or they might go for a slightly fluid skirt, which fits over the hips and flares out at the bottom, without adding bulk to the legs. **And their leather bags often have lots of edgy hardware like studs and zippers and metal appliqués.** If they were to copy their boss and buy a conservative logo status bag, at least it would be in glittery silver or orange, although they might well live to regret it.

Naughty Girls hate uniforms, but if the job requires it, they will alter theirs to fit perfectly.

If they have good legs, they will shorten their skirts as much as they can and wear heels as high as possible. They will then focus on hair and acceptable makeup and polish. **Men love lipstick.** Just because they don't want it on their shirt does not mean they are not into it. **Sometimes a red or berry or even bright pink shade of lipstick can really sex up a boring uniform look.**

Obviously, however, what is trashy in a school room might be acceptable at Hooters. At work, as much as anywhere, it's all about marketing and packaging yourself for the role you want to play and the setting of your performance. Whatever and wherever that is, go ahead, organize your closet and makeup drawer and get ready to turn up the heat.

Dump the losers

Everyone makes mistakes. Deep-six the following from your work closet:

If you have a big butt:

- ❤ High-waist pants, even if they are in fashion
- ❤ Pleated pants
- ❤ Short jackets

If you have big boobs:

- ❤ Tight, round-necked sweaters

Everyone should edit:

- ❤ Sweaters with baggy arms
- ❤ Skin-clinging tops

Nice Girl

There is nothing at all wrong with the way this Nice Girl looks at work.

She tries hard. Everyone in the office likes her well enough. In fact, Miss Naughty might hire her as an assistant.

Nonetheless, from her Nice Girl pink cashmere sweater set with real pearls to her beige bag and unsexy trousers, she melts right into the background.

I was with Jill when she blew her budget on the status bag because her boss had one in brown. Even though she purchased it at the outlet store, the money could have been better spent, in my opinion.

Trashy Girl

In most cases, work is the last place where you want to cross the line between sexy and slutty. You don't want to give everyone the wrong idea.

Remember, if a man thinks he has a chance at easy sex, he'll be much nicer, for awhile, but sooner or later he will get annoyed.

A rejected man, encouraged to hit on you because he thought you were going to be easy, is not a happy co-worker.

Tip: If people ask you all day long if you are going to a cocktail party later, it might not be a good thing.

❤ Extensions at work are naughty. Wigs at work are trashy, unless you are bald.

❤ The whole world is my gyno-micro-mini is trashy. If you are seated, with legs crossed, the skirt should not ride much shorter than half a hand's length from mid thigh.

❤ Long, long nails with spangles or flowers or funny designs are trashy.

❤ No more than a hint of cleavage, please. Tight sweaters and T-shirts, especially on big boobs are trashy.

The perfect jacket:
Fitted, deep V-neck
shows a flash of
color. Short length
of the jacket makes
legs look longer. →

Gold jewelry
to coordinate
with charms
and zippers
on her bag →

Little black
skirt, fitted,
but not tight ←

The wider the
skirt at the hem,
the slimmer the
legs will appear. ←

Naughty Girl

HOT PINK
is the
Naughty Girl's
black.

High-healed
latform pump →

The Naughty Girl's pants and sweater outfit at work:

❤ The sweater hugs her top and waist, hitting just at the hip.

❤ The pants are flattering to the butt and well fitted on the thighs, and hemmed long enough to cover a really high wedge shoe, so all you see is a great leg.

❤ The pants legs are designed with a flair and fall gracefully over her shoes or boots without stopping short or dragging to the ground.

Tip: Just because you feel bloated is no reason to resort to a stretch waistband skirt or pants with an oversized layered top. Instead, try a classic shift dress that goes with slides and a bare leg in warm weather or leggings in winter.

Naughty Girl's work closet:

❤ Perfectly fitted little black pantsuit. Pants paired with cute tops and the suit with soft blouses

❤ A flirty skirt

❤ Diane von Furstenberg wrap dress

❤ Pull-on boots, tight around the ankle and calf-length skirts in winter

❤ Socks and shoes coordinated with trousers or skirts to make legs look longer

❤ Coats with waists cut into them instead of trenches

❤ Tops: Ruched, wrapped to play up the waist. Deep V-necked sweaters over camisoles and undershirts

❤ White cotton shirt, slight V-neck, with turned up collar

❤ Cashmere sweater that fits nicely and is waist flattering, with length ending just at hip

❤ Wide-legged trousers with a lower waistline and loose fitting, because what naughty girl doesn't want to make her ass look smaller?

The Nice Girl
plays it safe
with nude and
tan and wears
the same face
every day.

The Trashy Girl
wears it all—nightclub
eyeshadows and bright
lipstick, thick, cakey,
artificial foundation.
Co-workers can't help
wondering if it's
all from the night
before.

Top
drawer
makeup
essentials
to keep
tucked
away:

❤ Lip glosses, one in
   a neutral lip tone
   and another in a
   perfect deep berry
   or red

❤ Great cotton and
   mineral loose
   powder makeup
   that is both sheer
   and translucent and
   offers sun block
   protection

The Naughty Girl has fun
changing her look, but her office
makeup, like her clothes, always
draws attention to one attribute at
a time. On one day, for instance,
she might wear a smoky heavy eye,
but with a natural nude glossy lip.
On another day, if she is in the
mood, a defined, fully colored lip
with great red lipstick, but with a
nude eyelid with mascara and liner.

Eye makeup for work:

1 Prepare the skin around your eyes with eye cream. Option: follow with **Insta-Fill for Eyes** to fill the fine lines and crow's feet and make a smooth surface before using concealer.

2 Apply concealer where necessary and blend. Skinn's **Bright Eyes-Eye Enhancing Treatment** is a light-weight, nourishing, self-adjusting concealer that is not wax based, so it doesn't look heavy and cakey. That's because the pigments used in this concealer reflect light away from the discoloration or dark circles and typically contain an orange base that will camouflage rather than try and cover the imperfection.

If not using concealer, apply an eyeshadow base before applying eyeshadow. It will help hide uneven skin tones, fill in lines, prevent creasing and protect the delicate eye tissues from pigments that may scratch.

3 Apply eyeliner or **Smudge Stick** and smudge with brush to blend. Everyone has a darker rim around the iris. Find eyeliner that matches that darkest edge and you have just found your go-to color. If you are in a hurry, don't use liquid eyeliner. It will ruin your day. Skinn's **Smudge Sticks** are ideal soft, smudgable eyeliners and are waterproof, so you can create sexy tear-rimmed eyes and smoky eyes that last all day.

Tip: When choosing among traditional heavy concealers, look for a formula that is based on a plant wax, such as Shea Butter. The formula will last longer without creasing.

Covering up

Before applying foundation, I often apply camouflage colors to act as a "correcting shade," such as green to balance red tones or yellow/orange to counteract blue (as in dark under eye circles). Another option is my **Orchid Gel Mattefying Day Treatment**. It can be used alone or under your makeup to keep your skin fresh, smooth and shine-free all day.

I apply concealer last, after camouflage colors and foundation. Choose a shade as close to, maybe half a shade lighter than your foundation. Apply the heavier concealer to all the areas you want to cover. My **Plasma Foundation** is offered with matching concealer and brush. Use a concealer brush that is round and pointed, in order to match the contours of the face.

3

Naughty First Date

The first date is a filtering process, the first elimination round.

During this time both of you will sniff each other out and decide whether you want a second date, based on the limited information you were able to obtain.

From what you could hear, see and sense, was this person bossy, pushy, blah, a gold digger, possibly mean, depressed, self-obsessed, neurotic, loaded with baggage or maybe some kind of weirdo? Or maybe he was perfectly nice, but....

The first date is also about experimenting with your chemistry together.

Do you like his smile? Do you feel good together? Is there a spark?

Nice Girls, like my friend Jill, see the first date as a job interview and/or a prelude to selecting their silver pattern and forget to relax and have a good time.

For Naughty Girls, however, the goal is to have fun and get asked out again. Then the ball is in their court, and they can decide whether to decline or accept, based on what they learned about the fellow and how much they liked them.

In the case of the majority of men, what they see of you in the beginning almost totally influences what they feel and believe about you. Eventually, the sexual spell wears off and the reverse is true: the way they feel about you will color the way you look to them. For those reasons, while I can't help you close the deal, **I can help you package and market yourself for the first date so that you will probably get asked for a second.**

Amp up the heat on makeup and dress to show him that this is an important occasion.

Make him want to kiss you.

During the date, you are taking in the heft of his shoulders, the friendliness and good humor in his gaze. He is experiencing the lilt of your voice, the come hither yet challenging look in your eyes. Hopefully, his eyes are also pouring over every curve of your body. So, this is the time, dare I say it, to **sacrifice comfort for glamour and va va vooom** and take extra care with your dress and makeup. **Give him something nice to look at, something pleasant to remember, and a hint of intriguing naughtiness that will pique his interest and make him want to come back for more.**

You say that the date has seen you many times before in your robe and slippers, taking out the garbage, for instance, or every weekday in your work clothes at the office elevators. If so, all the more reason to pick out something playful and flirty to wear that says, "I've been looking forward to spending a fun evening with you."

Many Naughty Girls I know say they prefer to play up one part of their body at a time on the first date.

For instance, if they show off a nice bosom with décolletage (not a bad idea for a dinner date), they won't wear a mini. They think of it as a strip tease. **The idea is to show a little bit of the body and make the guy wish he could see more.**

Some of the clothes that work well at the office are also great for the first date, except amp up the heat on makeup and dress to show him that this is an important occasion. No matter where you go, he wants to be proud to have you on his arm.

Then, if you think you like him, relax, flirt, have fun, use come hither body language if you are so inclined, challenge him conversationally in a light-hearted way that gives him a chance to come back at you. He wants a Nice Girl, but it is a glimpse of the naughty and flirtatious in you that will get and keep him interested enough to keep coming back to find out more about how nice you are.

Body language

Proven to encourage men:

- ♥ Caress your hair or subconsciously rub your wine glass. You might gently lick the rim of the glass. Avoid lipstick staining.

- ♥ Drop your voice so he has to lean in to hear you.

- ♥ Accidentally brush against him.

- ♥ Lean forward towards him.

- ♥ Smile and look him in the eyes.

- ♥ Mimic his body language and expression. Lean forward when he does, and backward when he does, showing you are in total sync.

- ♥ Touch his arm or leg when driving, sitting close to make a point in the conversation.

Nice and natural makeup doesn't set off smoke signals.

Cozy turtleneck makes her look lumpy.

The look should be kissable, not kiss-offable.

There is nothing wrong with the way the Nice Girl looks, if she is headed to a football game. "I don't want to look like I'm trying too hard," my friend Jill might say. A droopy fabric floral pin is her idea of adding spice.

Although what you wear depends on where you go, you shouldn't be afraid to look like you made an effort.

Dressing to impress is a compliment to him.

If you are too underdressed, he may take it as a sign you are not really interested. Don't you feel the same about the guy who comes to pick you up in his sloppy sweat pants?

Cuffed capri-length jeans cut off her legs.

Nice Girl

Flats add to stumpy look.

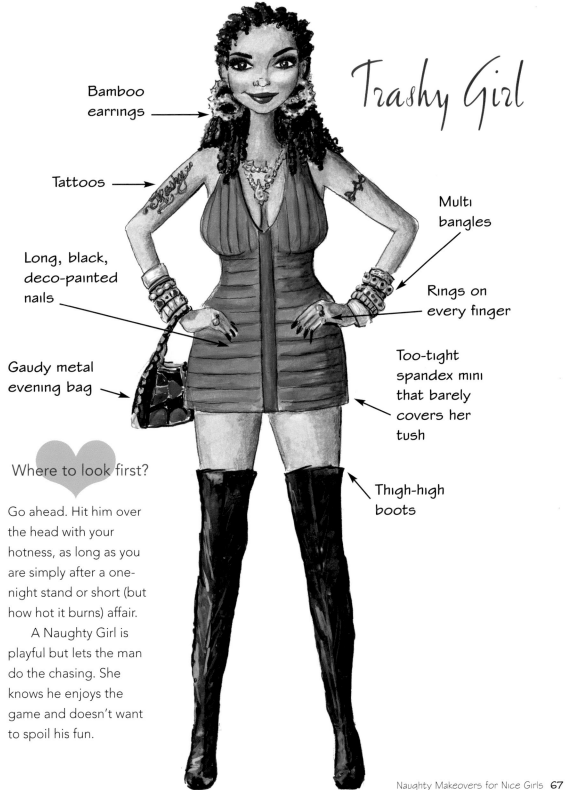

Trashy Girl

Bamboo earrings

Tattoos

Multi bangles

Long, black, deco-painted nails

Rings on every finger

Gaudy metal evening bag

Too-tight spandex mini that barely covers her tush

Thigh-high boots

Where to look first?

Go ahead. Hit him over the head with your hotness, as long as you are simply after a one-night stand or short (but how hot it burns) affair.

A Naughty Girl is playful but lets the man do the chasing. She knows he enjoys the game and doesn't want to spoil his fun.

Naughty Girl

A Nice Girl walks into a room as if to say, "Um. Here I am. Please notice me." A Naughty Girl saunters in, shoulders back, head held high, as if to say, "Here I am, world."

Believe me when I say that what you believe about the way you look is what people perceive. Looking pulled together and sexy will boost your confidence. To paraphrase Janis Joplin, "You'll know when you got it if it makes you feel good."

Gold jewelry to match envelope bag

Gold sequin sweater to throw over her shoulders

Beige platforms good to go with anything

Naughty Girl date night basics:

♥ Little shift dress with spaghetti straps and a cute little sweater you can take off

♥ High heels such as the nude platform pumps illustrated here

♥ Great fitting jeans with a high heel and cute silk crossover top

♥ A coat if it's cold, but not a blazer

♥ A top that is lace or sheer

♥ Black, wide-legged pants that fall over a high wedge shoe, coordinated with her perfectly fitting sweater that falls just below the waist

♥ She separates her twin sets and wears the cashmere cardigan unbuttoned low with a lacy camisole top peeping out.

Put your best face forward.

Say hello to him with your soft, smoky eyes and creamy natural-colored lips, your cheeks glowing with a clear flush of color.

Eyes: Choose a darker shade of smoky matte (i.e. dark plum, espresso, eggplant, bronze, gray, brownish green) and a complementary lighter shade to highlight.

Step 1: Using an angled liner or brow brush, line the entire eye with the darker shade of powder shadow.

Step 2: Apply the darker shade across the entire eyelid up to and into the orbital crease.

Step 3: Apply lighter shade under the eyebrow.

Step 4: Choose a **Smudge Stick** in a shade darker than or matching to the darker shade of eyeshadow. Apply eyeliner over the shadow and inside the lash lines (tear lines). Option: For a more subtle look, only use liner in the tear line and just leave the eyelid lined with the double layers of shadow. Lining the tear line is in and sexy.

Step 5: Fake eyelashes are bigger than ever. If you are hesitant about wearing them, try using individual lashes on the outer edge of your eyes. Choose a fiber-based mascara for better blending of fake and real lashes after fake lashes are applied.

Tip:

Cut the eyelash strips into segments and put them on. The outer corners always look great and it's worth the extra effort.

Lips: Choose a lipliner and a creamy satin finish, non-sparkly lipstick in a shade matching or just one shade lighter than the natural lip color.

Step 1: Begin by applying skin-tone matching mineral makeup all around the mouth and on the lips, using a brush.

Step 2: Apply lipliner just inside the lip line, then fill in the outer edges of the lower and upper lip, leaving the center untouched. The goal is an unlined "dimensional" look.

Step 3: Fill in lips with creamy, natural-toned lipstick. The center of the lips should be barely lighter than the edges.

Tip:

For a glossy look, skip the lipstick. Use a beige/nude gloss (without sparkle) with lipliner. Add mineral powder on lips for a perfect base.

You say your first date
is picking you up at work?
Here's how to make the transition
double quick.

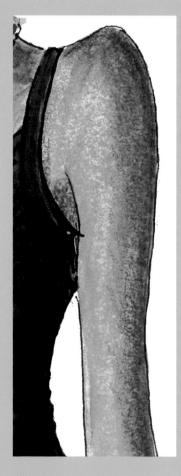

Eyes: Go ahead and
brush the same pink blush
over your eyelid on top of
your other eyeshadow. This
will instantly make your eyes
look sexy and softly focused.
Extend your black eyeliner
past the corner on your
upper lid so as to create a
sexy bat-wing look. Then,
apply a little soft blue
eyeliner from a shade of
silver periwinkle to a dark
indigo (whichever you like
best) in the lower inner
tear rims.

Body: Apply a
skin illuminating lotion
or powder to your
shoulders, arms and
legs. The subtle glow
will not only make you
feel and look sexier,
but the light reflecting
off your skin will flirt
for you all night long.

Face: First, powder your skin well with a very fine face powder and then lightly dust your complexion with a fine illuminating powder (available from most department and drugstore brands). This double layering of matte and illuminating powders will result in a naturally smooth and glowing finish that will respond well to candlelight. Next, blush your cheeks with an iridescent pink blush.

Lips: This may be the perfect occasion for that red lipstick you fear every other day. Red lipstick really emphasizes your skin. First, line your lips with a red liner since red can easily highlight an uneven lip line and has a tendency to be unforgiving when it comes to feathering. A red liner will keep your lips and lip line looking perfect. After applying lipstick, finish with a sheer icy reflective gloss over your lipstick, and you'll look and feel sultry and sexy.

Naughty Online

What's that? You say you are not hooked into social media? You don't even have an iPhone?

Honey, come out of your cave. I'm driving right over to stage an intervention.

If you are single and looking for men, you are missing the boat if you don't try an online dating service like eHarmony.com and Match.com. Sure you'll meet more losers than winners, but the elimination process is much more efficient and painless from your point of view. And it offers the opportunity to flirt safely online and look over prospects you would never meet cruising bars or hanging at Starbucks.

If you are happy and involved, there are still all those Facebook and LinkedIn type sites used by everybody for professional and social reasons, such as keeping up with and finding old friends or making needed contacts and obtaining information.

No matter how you might protest, online connecting requires uploading at least one good recent photo of yourself. And do I even need to tell you to never put a photo of yourself on the social media that you don't want a potential employer or your grandma to see? That does not mean that even for your picture on professional sites, you can't look foxy and interesting. And of course, this is exactly the impression you want to convey on dating sites.

To be on a magazine cover, a model or gorgeous celebrity puts in an 8-hour day. She is all tricked out by the top makeup and hair people. She is dressed to kill in the best money can buy by a stylist who clothespins and tapes the clothes to fit her perfectly. The photographer gets the lighting just right, usually with the help of an assistant. Hundreds of pictures are taken, and eventually these are narrowed down to maybe 5 to10 for a team of nitpickers to edit. The celebrity may have final approval and retouching rights, which means the picture will be altered to remove wrinkles, circles, whatever.

> The false advertising photo is the number one complaint I hear about Internet dating from both men and women.

You may not want to go to that extreme. You want your picture to look like a reasonable facsimile of yourself so the guy won't feel he has been duped. You should accept that some men will find you attractive and others will not. Nonetheless, you also want to take the time to present the best online visual image possible.

If you are going on a dating service, remember, **the pictures should be something that you in the flesh can live up to now**, and not be you 5 years and 20 pounds ago. When offering more than one picture, always include at least one that shows your body. If not, the man will assume you have something to hide.

> Don't pretend to be something you are not and figure you'll win him over with your personality.

Sandy is a lot of laughs but has been about 70 pounds overweight all her life. She has a pretty face and shows herself from neck up on dating websites. At the first meet, she drapes a shawl around her shoulders, so she looks not so fat across the table at a restaurant. She hopes this gives her a chance to win him over with her personality, but it never works. Instead, **the guy feels deceived by a woman who misrepresented herself.** I constantly tell her that every pot has a lid and there are many young, good looking, nice guys who are crazy for large women. She'd be far better off owning it and advertising herself as a woman who embraces her curves, including photographs that show her silhouette.

Video tips:

The Internet is the way I sell my cosmetics. It's the way many people do business. You may find yourself making streaming Internet videos yourself someday, just like I did, so I am offering a few video lessons that I learned the hard way. These might also come in handy for those Skype interviews.

- ❤ Don't wear the same color clothes as your background.

- ❤ Be sure the direct lighting is not up or down. Either one casts strange shadows.

- ❤ Use heavier makeup because the camera washes you out. That means you need to give a sharper edge to your eyes and lips and use more blush and bronzer.

- ❤ Cameras make your hair look flat. This is the one time and place where backcombing the crown is a good idea.

- ❤ Fitted clothes look better than loose and flouncy. Make sure your sleeves are slender.

- ❤ Look at the camera and focus. Pretend like you are speaking to someone.

- ❤ Use eye drops to brighten the whites of your eyes.

The false advertising photo is the number one complaint I hear about Internet dating from both men and women. This is not to say you shouldn't take the time to pose for and choose the right pictures that show you to your best advantage.

For dating sites, four photos is probably a good number. Although one head shot is nice to give a close-up of your face, at least some of them should show your body.

Think of all the situations we talk about in this book—going on the first date, hanging out at home, running to the market and around the neighborhood, going to church, vacationing.

Once you get yourself together, start carrying a camera around with you for all these situations, and on days when you have it all together, get a friend to take pictures. The more situations you have to choose from, the better. **Anything that shows you having fun and being natural is great.** Then edit the results down to four.

Although photographs of you at work are fine for professional networking, do not be tempted to include them on dating sites.

Leslie Oren, a foxy friend, now the bride of a charming architect, not long ago wrote a fun and informative book about Internet dating, *Fine, I'll Go Online: The Hollywood Publicists Guide to Successful Internet Dating*. It takes you through every step of the process, including writing and responding to ads. A friend took a killer shot of Leslie in her beautifully decorated office. Her hair was just right that day, the makeup perfect, her outfit "stylishly professional." The sun streamed in through the window in just the right way for beautiful natural lighting. It was so flattering; she couldn't help but include it in her mix. (She says any more than four photos are overkill).

The good news is that she heard from many desirable guys. But they all wanted to network. She ended up giving free business advice, offering leads, propping up weakened egos and even writing a resume.

Of course, that same photo of her is dynamite on a professional networking site. **But your online dating photos**, she says, **should show you off as "lovely, warm, happy, adventurous, open and feminine—** not the traits one immediately associates with work."

Leslie suggests current happy photos that show you looking like you're having fun, photos that show you dressed up for a night on the town and outside or on vacation, when you're in a beautiful setting and look relaxed. Candids of you looking cute with your pet or gardening or relaxing around your house are also good. So is being dressed to do something athletic, like playing tennis or riding a bicycle or skiing, but only if you have a real interest in the activity.

Nice Girl

Guaranteed turn-offs, no matter how great you look

1 You holding a baby. My friend Jill is on several dating sites. She always includes a photo of her as Auntie Jill, holding her sister's baby, so men think she would be a good mother. Nothing makes a man run faster. You might as well scream, "Make me pregnant."

2 A picture of you as a bridesmaid, standing next to six other girls, all dolled up. In fact, it's wise not to send any pictures of you posed with good-looking female friends. Why distract the fish before it takes the bait?

3 Also forget pictures taken with your best male gay friend or a relative, no matter how hot you looked that night. Even if one of these guys was never your boyfriend, the man viewing the picture will suspect he was. It will be a turn off.

Guaranteed
to spark response.

Trashy Girls and Naughty Girls
too, have been known to use
Halloween parties and other such
occasions as an excuse to dress
in garb designed to tickle male
fantasies. That's fine, but don't
upload such pictures of yourself
to a dating site. Not in Halloween
costumes, lingerie or any other
such garb. You'll attract plenty of
men, but what are you going to
do with them, and how are you
going to get rid of them?

And don't forget what I said
about never posting a picture on
the Internet without realizing it
might be seen by your potential
employer, mother-in-law, etc.

Trashy Girl

Naughty Girl

Wish you were here.

If you have it, flaunt it. Include at least one shot to show off your bodacious bod, if you have one. But don't make it look like you are posing for a picture. It should show you're having fun, in a natural setting. You can be wearing a bikini, for instance, if you are having fun at the beach and/or on a resort vacation.

Tips for taking a good photo:

❤ Think of something naughty and smile with your eyes.

❤ Pay attention to your lighting. Indirect natural lighting is most flattering. Do not pose with the sun glaring directly at you, above you or behind you.

❤ For a thinner looking face the photo should be captured from above and with the camera angled down towards you. Look upwards with your eyes and not your head.

Makeup tips:

Get ready for your close-ups

❤ Use matte finish bronzer to contour a full face, double chin or crooked nose. Matte makeup that is slightly darker than your natural shade sculpts like a chisel when placed beneath cheek-bones, under jaw line or on sides of your nose.

❤ Use silicone matte primer, such as Skinn's Orchid Gel Mattefying Day Treatment, which smoothes out pores and imperfections.

❤ Avoid makeup with a metallic or pearl sheen. It doesn't photograph well.

❤ To make lips look soft and supple, try Skinn's Three-Minute Lip Party Rapid Volumizing Mask.

❤ Exfoliate and moisturize lips, then line with a neutral shade, close to your natural color. Extend the lipliner to the lip line and fill in with matte lipstick or colored gloss.

❤ Before uploading to Facebook or a dating site, you could use basic photo editing software such as Photoshop to brighten, sharpen, blur and remove blemishes.

Naughty Cougars

It's no longer just Demi Moore, Madonna and Cher.

Hot Mamas with younger men are everywhere I look. And it's not just a Sugar Mommy thing either. The sexual attraction is mutual, and there are websites to prove it.

You're not susceptible to younger men? What one learns from these Cougars can benefit anyone interested in looking younger.

That would be all of us. **Age is our common enemy, and we're not going to give in without a fight.** Every woman knows that looking younger will keep her on the job and in the game longer.

The Palm Springs desert area, where I reside, is teeming with smoking-hot Cougars, well over 50; some are widowed and well heeled, some still working women. They are very high end with their strappy gladiators and off-shoulder tops, everything beautifully put together.

They prefer younger men because the older men, they say, are looking for "a nurse with a purse."

My neighborhood bar in the Palm Springs area is a meeting place for these Cougars and marines from a nearby base in 29 Palms. Local young women on the prowl also come here looking to connect, and many a night I've enjoyed the show as they flaunt their store-bought racks and rears in the tightest tops and shortest skirts possible. **Nine times out of ten, the Cougars get the men.** These soldiers aren't looking for Sugar Mommies, but a hot night, and cougars are known to be sophisticated, attractive, sexually hip and in control.

To find out their youthful secrets, I turned to Nicole, my very chic French friend. Like a typical French woman, she insists on "an unlisted age," but appears to be in her early 40s. However, I happen to know that she came to the U.S. in her early 20s and has been representing a Paris-based corporation in Los Angeles for the past 38 years, working herself up from assistant to West Coast director. I also know that she rejoices in the vibe of being with a younger man. To my mind, she is the image of a Naughty Cougar.

"Cougar sounds so predatory," she said, objecting to the title of this chapter. **"There are many reasons women turn to younger men during different stages of their lives, and it goes way beyond the longing for a whiff of fresh meat."**

Nicole is very French in her approach and describes herself as "a high priestess on love's food chain." In her early years, she benefitted from the experience of an older man, and now she is returning the favor.

> The older men, they say, are looking for a nurse with a purse.

While she keeps fit and toned, the men in her age group are pudgy and out of shape. "And, even though they have the big pot belly and hair out their ears, the 62-year-old man still wants the 35-year-old hard body."

A woman who has worked hard at looking great deserves a guy who is equally fit as well as enthusiastic.

When Nicole dates a man 20 years younger—and she has, off and on, throughout her life—no one really notices the age disparity. She has sparkly eyes and a luxurious mane of brown, shoulder-length, wavy hair that is subtly highlighted with gold. Her skin is peachy, her body is taut. She has not veered from her trim 115-pound, 5' 5" frame since she was a girl. She has the French appreciation of food, but she also began working out at nine—dance, acrobatics and more. And currently she is taking private yoga and puts in overtime for the arms, doing adult gymnastics, working on a trapeze and pumping iron.

For six years, she was pole dancing, a combination of yoga and gymnastics, with Sheila Kelley S Factor.

She is high maintenance. She maintains her skin by regularly going to a trusted dermatologist for a series of light glycolic acid peels and microdermabrasions.

She also exfoliates frequently at home, with my **DermAppeal Microdermabrasion Treatment**.

Before a big date, she says she exfoliates her entire body with my **Smooth & Sweet Sugar Scrub**, so her skin is smooth and soft to the touch, and then applies a self tanner.

And she gets eyelash extensions so she can go without makeup and still look fabulous. The beauty budget also includes gel manicures every three weeks.

It's not easy staying fabulous.

"**I'm spending a lot more time and money looking natural,**" she says with a wry smile. "The old wooden boat needs love and attention and a lot of good maintenance."

Like Nicole, the typical Naughty Cougar has to put in time to maintain a toned body, younger look and hotter fashion attitude than other women of her years. **Hair dye, collagen and fillers are her best friends.**

From Botox to fillers to peels to lasers, there are so many noninvasive options to wrinkle management, and I've used some of them myself. However, whether or not you choose to see a dermatologist, becoming fanatic about daily skin care is now essential.

Aging Looks

- Pierced earring and hole hangs from years of being stretched open

- Back bra fat from too tight of a bra or shirt

- Discolored and/or worn-down teeth

- Nude lips. Brighter shades, brick red or brighter peachy or pinkish shades on the brighter side tend to de-age. Soft pearlized lip shades make women look younger.

- Frosted eyeshadow. Lightly pearlized, on the other hand, makes you look younger.

- Thick black eyeliner and cracked liquid liner

- Clumpy mascara

- One strip of fake eyelashes

- Too much color in the shadow

- Any fashion that shows off body parts not in shipshape, such as low-cut blouses revealing cleavage that is wrinkled and sun damaged.

- Baggy pants or jeans

- Droopy breasts. Make sure your bra will boost you halfway between your shoulders and elbows, or do not leave the house.

Bright blue eyeshadow

Thick line of eyeliner

Bustier with boobs pushed out

Lots of glitzy jewelry

Long fingernails

Trashy Cougar

We've all seen women, on television and elsewhere, who take their efforts to a frightening extreme to become caricatures of their former selves with fat silicone-puffed lips over-lifted faces, bleached-out hair and clothes that are way too young. I saw just such a Cougar yesterday at my dermatologist's office, with puffed-out lips and over-lifted face. Her low-cut yoga pants and workout bra revealed a stick-like body with huge boobs and a belly ring. Her prosperous-looking young boyfriend was with her. "He's paying for this," she told the office assistant," while all the other patients in the waiting room looked on, mouths dropped.

Off-shoulder
top shows off
her beautiful
shoulders.

Brown
wavy hair
streaked
with gold

Pendant on
a long chain
is figure
flattering.

Slim
cigarette
pants

Naughty Cougar

High heels
show her ass.

The Naughty Cougar knows all about makeup and how to use it.

You'll never see her take out the trash without all her makeup on. You'll also never see this classy lady dangle eyeglasses on a chain around her neck, allow her teeth to yellow or let her boobs hang down to her waist. However, unlike the Trashy Cougar, she takes care to present herself at her best rather than grabbing willy nilly at the fashions favored by younger women.

Shoulders look young at any age, and the Cougar chooses her best features to show off.

The Naughty Cougar knows that clothing that is really age inappropriate and doesn't flatter the figure only emphasizes the difference between her age and the "young look." She is also realistic about what needs to be covered up. If it's upper arms, and it inevitably is after a certain age, she knows how to disguise it with crochet tops and shrugs. If she has a wrinkled chest, she avoids deep décolletage and owns thick necklaces that cover the area. On the other hand, if she has an unlined bosom and beautiful shoulders, she shows them with strapless tops and tanks and doesn't worry that the look is too young.

A Naughty Cougar over 60 does not wear shoes that hurt her feet, artificial fingernails in bright colors, too much jewelry, matchy-matchy clothes or jeans that are so tight that they hurt her frou frou. She knows visible elastic waistbands age her, but they are comfortable if you keep them covered. And looking comfortable is sexy.

When she goes out with a younger man and his friends, Nicole never dresses in clothes from the office. Instead she picks sexy designer jeans and little sporty crop polo shirt, worn with little pointy sexy sandals or Pumas, sometimes jeans tucked into high heeled boots. With it she adds a really gorgeous belt or another nice looking accessory. "I am not a slave to fashion, and though I'm happy to be stylish, I don't spend a lot on clothes. For me it's about keeping toned and fit, flexible and slender."

Shoulders look young at any age, and the Cougar chooses her best features to show off.

Bedside: The Naughty Cougar keeps a lubricant hidden under the bed. A fabulous lubricant, a knowledgeable friend told me, is Astroglide.

Daily beauty ritual for younger looking skin:

Cleanse:
Morning: Sulfate Free Gentle Exfoliating Cleanser.
Evening: Olive & Enzyme Rich Balm Cleanser.

Exfoliate:
Dermappeal Microdermabrasion Treatment.

Restore:
Collagenesis Stem Rejen Sirtuin Support Facial Contour Lifting Serum for the face and Stem Rejen Eye Serum.

Moisturize:
Collagenesis Twenty-Four Hour Youth Preservation.

Protect:
Skinnsurance SPF 30.

All about hair

Hair dye and bangs are among a Naughty Cougar's best friends.

Gray ages a woman. Going back to a few shades lighter than the original color is the best approach. Be sure hair color is not too dark. That doesn't mean everyone should be blond, but brunettes could be soft and subtly highlighted. A solid block of hair is not so good. **Subtle gold highlights, carefully placed to frame the face will soften your look.**

Women who do go with dark hair should have strong features and/or wear enough makeup so that their face does not fade to pale by comparison.

Bangs make every woman look younger, but don't call them that in the U.K. and Australia, where it means having sex. Call it a fringe. (And if you are in those countries, don't ask for a shag haircut, especially not a shag with heavy bangs.) I'm sorry to have to tell you that big hair is aging. Back-combed hair is aging. Hair that doesn't move because it is sprayed stiff is aging. So are those bumps put under the crown to make it poufy. **Smooth hair is younger.** And the fastest way to make mistakes and age yourself is to do it yourself. I've said it before, and I'll say it again. If you want to look younger, save somewhere else and go to a good hair stylist.

Naughty in the Hood

What do people think and say about you?

Just imagine you are naughty enough, maybe even zany enough, to call your neighbors posing as a cop.

You question them about yourself and hint you may be a person of interest in a recent crime. Based on how they see you around the hood all the time, what do you imagine they might say about you? Bag Lady? Moody Mummy? Mutton Dressed Like Lamb? Suspicious Character? Possible Dealer?

Or, even worse, do they not remember you at all and therefore can't verify that when the crime took place, you were sitting at the counter of the pancake place across the street from your house, just like you always are every freaking Saturday morning.

Show street smarts.

You say you take enough pains on your looks at work, you want to let things slide on weekends, veg out a little. Believe me, I understand. But remember, **it's when you relax your standards and look your worst that you run into the last person you want to see.**

I know Jill through my long-time friend, her aunt Lulu, a person of influence in the world of fashion and beauty. The first year after Jill was graduated from college, she lived with Lulu in her childhood neighborhood. That was about six years

Nice Girl

Jill, my Nice Girl, often runs around all weekend in workout wear, but her loose jacket covers her up, rather than showing off her waistline.

The other day, I met Jill at our neighborhood breakfast spot. This time she was in baggy jeans and a T-shirt, leather flip flops, a short jean jacket. I couldn't refrain from telling her that denim jackets and pants are not meant to be worn together. And loose sloppy jeans and an old T-shirt or sweatshirt are not enticing!

Another Nice Girl look that is not sexy is baseball hats. Men will never approach a woman in a baseball hat, especially if they can't see her eyes. Ponytails without a hat are better.

ago, and I remember Lulu reporting that Jill and her gal pals went to the local theater and to the store in flannel pajama bottoms and thermal underwear tops, usually without bras. They even wore their slippers out with their pajamas when they met at the neighborhood coffee shop.

Would you believe it? They'd get all glammed up for a trip to Los Angeles, but they couldn't be bothered for their own neighborhood in suburbia.

For the true Naughty Girl, looking like a total babe is a lifestyle choice. Women put so much effort into dressing up for a night out, but how often do they really ever fall in love (or vice versa) with the men they meet at clubs? The men they encounter in real life, casual day-to-day experiences are much more likely to be suitable partners.

On a recent Saturday, I met my dishy French friend Nicole over a skinny latte at Starbucks. She was cozy, elegant and sexy in a loose, lush, black velvet shirt, ankle-length Chinese brocade green, black and gold pants and black patent leather ballet shoes.

What are French women wearing to run errands around the Right Bank these days? "Little shift dresses," Nicole, reported. "At every turn their first choice is some form of dress or a skirt with a tank and a cardigan. **Denim is only big big big in London and here.** In Paris you cannot be taken seriously if you show up in designer jeans and a T-shirt. A French woman would not wear cut-off denims, thermal tights or anything thermal. They consider tights with over-sized T-shirts and boots in very poor taste."

Phooey on the Right Bank women. No matter what they disdain, **the look of tights with a mini dress is a great variation on the dress, especially with boots and heels.** And no matter what your age, especially in the winter, you can't beat a good pair of jeans that make you look great and are comfortable. If they meet both criteria, they are worth their weight in gold. And white jeans go a long way in the summer, worn with white T-shirts.

My young publicist, Lauren, says that she would not be caught wearing frumpy sweat pants, chunky heels, Birkenstocks, Juicy Couture, anything with puff paint, anything that has a cutesy phrase or a large logo. "Why be anybody's billboard?" And she adds, she doesn't wear gym clothes unless she is coming or going to the gym.

When she runs errands, it's in straight-leg jeans with a white T-shirt or tank top and a cashmere cardigan or jacket. In the summer, she might wear denim or cuffed khaki shorts (never, ever with cargo pockets) or a cute skirt, knee-length to mid-thigh. For shoes, she likes ballet flats, flat boots or leather flip flops (never, ever the plastic kind you find at the beach). She carries a large, chic tote that can hold everything and always brings a colorful re-usable grocery bag along with her wherever she goes.

Workout wear where?

She is one fashionista who changes into street clothes as soon as she leaves her gym. I suppose, when you are in your 20s, you have the time and energy to pack a duffel bag and change 10 times a day. But for most dishy women I know, life is not a traveling fashion shoot.

There's nothing wrong with workout clothes on the street, as long as they flatter your assets. If you are wearing a yoga or workout outfit, make sure it is well fitting and of good quality like Lululemon, www.lululemon.com, Nicole's favorite brand. "The jackets are slenderizing and have enough thickness to keep me warm."

When sandal season comes, make sure your feet are well kept with no visible dead skin or cracks on your heels. Toenails should be well manicured with a fun color polish or something clean, like a French manicure.

"I don't understand how a woman can leave the house without fixing herself up a little—if only out of politeness, "My idol, Coco Chanel, said, "Maybe that's the day she has a date with destiny. And it's best to be as pretty as possible for destiny."

Remember, you never get a second chance to make a first impression. Always present yourself in the way you want others to perceive you.

I always shower and fix my hair before going to the gym. Don't you?

Trashy Girl

Not good in the hood:

- ❤ Daisy Mae cut-off jeans, even if you've got great stems

- ❤ Short shorts that reveal cellulite or veins

- ❤ Looking like you are trying too hard

- ❤ Cleavage all out and pushed up under a low top

- ❤ Enough jewelry to arouse suspicion that you are a shoplifter

Naughty Girl

The sexiest accessory you can wear every day is a great inviting smile. Most men are intimidated and uncomfortable about approaching a woman, and a smile makes it easier. For that matter, even a smile with a hello doesn't cost you anything.

Add to that a cute, loosely tied, bright scarf over a T-shirt and try a little higher heel under a pair of well-fitting jeans.

For extra glam with little to no effort, don a pair of diamond stud earrings or a fun necklace or bracelet.

It's all about details. Carry a cute purse and make sure it is not tattered, worn out or dirty looking. A worn-out bag will ruin any outfit.

What if you have no time to bother with your hair?

Makeup tips:

Refer to your basic five-minute makeup, page 38. Don't leave home without it if you are over 25.

Even my 23-year-old niece will plump up and refresh her skin with Skinn's Collagenesis, dot on a little concealer under her eyes, curl her lashes and swipe on 2 to 3 coats of black mascara. She adds to that a bit of blush. Skinn's Color Touch Eye, Cheek & Lip Glow in Golden Peach is her favorite.
"I like to look alive and awake."

She has one cardinal rule.
"I never leave the house without mascara."

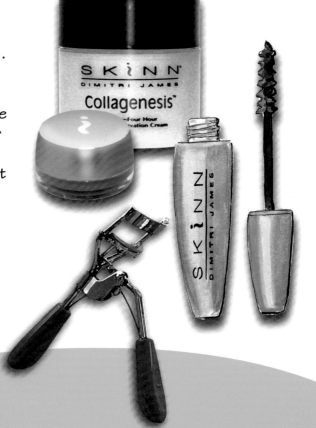

Nicole washes or at least wets her hair, applies conditioner and slicks it straight back in her simple version of a chignon or ponytail. When she does this, she adds lots of eye makeup.

The same can be done, of course, with short hair, but why bother? A good short cut should dry naturally and look great.

If you don't have the option of a ponytail or loose chignon/bun, tortoise shell hair clips also work wonders if your hair is long enough.

And then, there is always a casual, slouchy hat that covers your hair but not your face.

7

Naughty at Home

Two's company.

When I arrived at Jill's house with a sausage and mushroom pizza last month, she greeted me in her old Bruin T-shirt over sweatpants, no makeup, and stringy hair tucked behind her ears. Papers and magazines were strewn all over the coffee table in front of the television where we were going to watch *Sex in the City 2*. The living room was an uninviting mess, and so was she.

To tell you the truth, I was miffed.

I had showered, slapped on Prada Infusion for Men and was wearing linen pants and a nice shirt. We hadn't seen each other for weeks. I was looking forward to catching up and had made an extra effort to drive out of the way to get her favorite designer pizza, parking my Mercedes in a risky part of town. She knew I was coming, and at least she could have run a comb through her hair and brushed her teeth.

"I hope you don't dress that way when you have lovers over?" I couldn't refrain from saying.

"Don't be mean. I work so hard during the week. I need to chill when I am at home." She yawned, like she had just gotten out of bed and was sorry to be woken up.

"Women have no idea how bad they can look when they slip into that comfort zone."

She flinched, and I could see I had hit a mark. "This is how I dress with my girlfriends. We all look like this when we relax and let down our hair," she said in a hurt tone.

Like many young women, her weekend fashion at home is a carryover from her college days, when she hung out in the sorority house with her Delta sisters wearing Greek sweatshirts and oversized, stained sweatpants. Footwear of choice was and is usually Birkenstocks, raggedy men's socks and worn out Uggs. **Ugh.**

With so many women, it's either all or nothing. They go to great lengths to look fabulous when they go out with their mate. But when they are at home with him, which is most of the time, they let themselves go.

Men are very visual.

If your guy sees you all the time walking around the house in old sweats that are baggy in the butt and make you look like a frump, that's the way he will start to remember you, and not the great way you looked on the one night when you were all dolled up.

I believe that women who take better care of themselves and don't get lazy and sloppy about their looks, tend to have better relationships. The better you look at home, the more respect you will get from whoever is with you. That includes yourself.

Nice Girl

Nice Girls should learn that lingerie is as much a female aphrodisiac as anything.

Knowing you are choosing to wear something to make him hot will turn you on as well. **And men adore sexy lingerie.** You don't have to be thin and/or in great shape. Women of all sizes look gorgeous in it. If you don't believe me, try to pry your *Agent Provocateur* catalog out of his strong hands and check out sites like www.secretsinlace.com.

The worse thing to happen to Jill and other women I know was the invention of those horrid blankets with arms. Jill wears hers with flannel Lanz pajamas. She was already a blooming couch potato and a slug, but her idea of a heaven these days is a cozy Saturday night with pizza, a movie and her Snuggie fleece blanket.

True Naughty Girls make it their lifestyle to look their best, even if they are alone.

It's especially easy to let go, especially when working at home. You go to check your e-mails on the computer with coffee in the morning, and before you know it, the day is over and you are still in your T-shirt and pajama bottoms, with an old terrycloth hoodie pulled over for warmth.

I asked my Naughty Girl friends how they get comfy at home. They all confessed to removing jeans and constricting garments the moment they could. "You have to give the hoo-ha a breather."

But cozy doesn't have to mean slug-like. Light, loose cotton shirts and pants in matching colors or dresses, all of which can easily be washed at home, are ideal.

Nicole lounges around in James Perse knit lounge pants and matching camisoles with built-in bras. For staying in for dinner and a movie with her lover, she wears a sexy black full slip with a cashmere shawl, silk classic pajamas or long lounge pants in flowing fabric with a tank top that matches.

You are insulting your friends, platonic and otherwise, if you make no attempt to groom yourself and your home when they come over for a scheduled visit.

Even if you are not in perfect shape, you can still wear a bra and thong or booty type shorts with silky robe.

When someone comes to your house, have it clean and inviting, with candles burning, maybe a tray set up with grapes and cheese, and the lights dimmed.

It's a way to say "I like you. I am looking forward to spending time with you and I put some effort into getting ready."

Even if you are flying solo for the weekend, you could do and say the same thing to yourself.

Cozy and casual need not mean slovenly and unappealing. You do have your friend in the mirror. If she looks good, you'll feel good.

The power of lingerie

Never underestimate the power of lingerie over men. There is a little Dita Von Teese in every Naughty Girl. And Dita is a very, very Naughty Girl. She is a class act, brilliantly exploiting the power of alluring lingerie of every conception, including elaborate items such as corsets and basques, playsuits, knickers, garters with hose and fully fashioned stockings.

You don't have to go that far. Just hanging out for a naughty weekend with the man in your life could be as simple as booty shorts and a tank top if you have a good bod, pajama bottoms and camisoles, lacy or silky shorts, and long kimonos or flowing robes.

Even if you are not in perfect shape, you can still wear a bra and thong or booty-type shorts with silky robe, maybe knee-length, over it. Even if it doesn't show, you know it's there. **Cross your legs and move around, and flash a bit of lingerie. It's very hot.**

And why not lounge around in slinky and silky robes, light gowns and pajamas. They are just as comfortable as sweats, really, and they look gorgeous.

If you got great boobs, by all means, don't wear a bra, but if you sag, go for some support with camisoles and negligees that feature built-in bras.

My newlywed friend wears risqué underwear at all times and has thrown away every pair of cotton panties she owned, especially the ones with logo elastic waistbands. "Men don't like them, and they are not flattering ever."

Female friends polled on this issue were divided. Nude and even sheer intimates also have their place, of course, mainly under clothes. **However, every woman should have a sexy pair of matching hot pink, black or red bras and panties for show and tell.** Don't worry how they will look under your white blouse. These are meant to be worn at home for amour.

Beer is not as sexy as a vodka martini.

Camel toe is a no no, even at home.

Trashy Girl

A Naughty Girl knows the power of lingerie and is willing to live out fantasies, as long as she can remain classy and respected. I wouldn't put any kind of lingerie past a True Naughty Girl, and I'm talking about costumes out of *Agent Provocateur* as well as Victoria's Secret, maybe Frederick's of Hollywood.

Some Very Naughty Girls see nothing unusual about owning elaborate lingerie and costumes including teddies, bustiers, corsets, garters, fluffy heels, naughty nurse outfits, crotchless panties, whips with ribbon tassels and every male fantasy garment that helps get things going. That includes fabulous wigs in assorted lengths and colors. After all, if he is going to be with a woman, it might as well be you.

Naughty Girl

Way up

If you want to pull your hair back in a ponytail, be aware it looks younger when it's higher and on top of your head.

Bare faced

The bare minimum makeup, even if you are home alone, is mascara and lip enhancers. My Twin Set Collagen Boost Lipstick & Wet Lips Gloss does the job.

Eyelashes

I understand not wearing mascara to bed, but if your eyelashes are pale, I recommend you get them tinted black. If you do sleep with mascara, make sure it is waterproof.

Sick leave

Even if you are home alone with the flu, there is no reason to let down on your standards. If you throw up, at least stop and brush your teeth, splash water on your face and put on some moisturizer. Believe me, it's as good as chicken soup for making you feel better.

Bare necessities, even when you are at home alone

8

Naughty Traveler

Let's be honest. The Naughty Girl has a lot of baggage, especially if there is a man around to carry it.

As I write this, my Nice Girl neighbor Laura is on a three-month European expedition with her hunky husband, a retired cop and very capable of heavy lifting.

At his suggestion, they each took a rolling carry-on that was slim enough to fit in the overhead bin. That was it. For three months. Being a Nice Girl, she went along with this program.

Most Naughty Girls would not easily agree to backpack around Europe with their mates. A rolling carry-on bag would not get them through a two-day business trip, let alone three months. They might have gypsy in their soul, but they need a caravan to carry their suitcases. They have to have options.

"I think it's a good idea to have a suitcase just for shoes," suggested my dear friend, Olivia Haley from Nolensville, Tennessee, when asked if she had any packing tips for this book. "When your shoes are all in one place, it's so much more organized."

Olivia also suggested carrying a suitcase dedicated to makeup and beauty products. Crowned Ms. Senior America in 2008, she does not step out of her ranch unless she is in full makeup and, very probably, wearing high heels. She is absolutely gorgeous and stands out in every crowd. She works in commercials, print ads and videos and is always dressed and made up, wherever she goes. Sure, her husband of 48 years complains. She doesn't waiver. She enjoys being this way and always packs lots of options. "I want to make the decision about what to wear after I get there."

Phyllis, a sophisticated, glamorous blonde, has no problem on the many Seabourn and Crystal Cruises she goes on with her long-time mate. They are both former New Yorkers, and he enjoys dressing up as much as she does.

> I'd rather schlep too much stuff than be caught without the perfect thing to wear.

Her fashion-ready packing techniques are not so good for business traveling, however, especially with her bad back. She owns her own company on the West Coast and for the past 15 years has been shuffling between New York and Los Angeles almost every month.

I was delighted to bump into her a few

months ago at the JFK luggage bin. We were on the same flight, but I hadn't seen her because she had flown First Class.

As usual, she stood out from the black-suited crowd in a lime-green pantsuit with turquoise jewelry. We exchanged kisses, talked about mutual friends in the beauty industry and decided to share a cab to the city. Phyllis was in New York for three days and planned a presentation to a major corporation. Besides her carry-on, filled mostly with cosmetics and medicine, she checked in a garment bag and medium-sized suitcase, and was defensive when I teased her about her luggage.

She loves bright colors and brought a red suit with fashionable details for the meeting. For nights out with friends, she packed one blouse and two alternative sweaters to wear with the red suit, backup pants and jacket and two dresses.

"I have to have options. What if something gets spilled on my jacket? What if it rains and I only have expensive shoes or suede pants with me? I'd rather schlep too much stuff than be caught without the perfect thing to wear."

To lighten the load, the obvious solution is to focus on one color.

Of course, where you go, be it the tropics or Istanbul, determines your color scheme as well as choices. If you are headed for a

What not to pack on your European vacation:

- ❤ Bermuda shorts
- ❤ Tennis shoes
- ❤ Backpacks
- ❤ Hippie sandals
- ❤ Visors
- ❤ Fanny packs
- ❤ T-shirts with collars
- ❤ Real jewelry

Tip:

Copy all documents, credit cards and prescriptions. Look into Skype for inexpensive and free calls. Book hotels in advance.

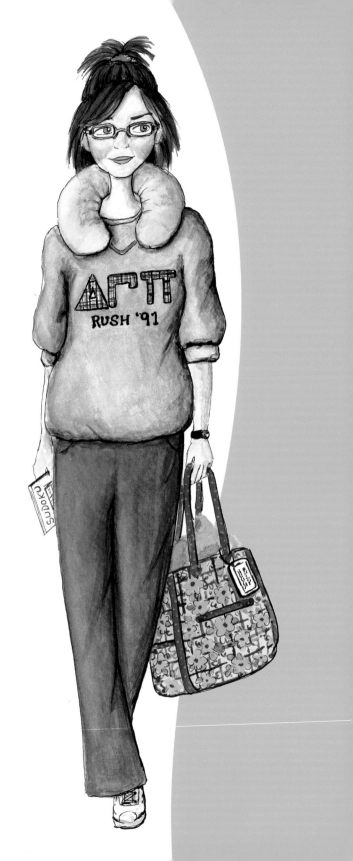

resort, bikinis and cover-ups are space savers, white and a color is great, and on your return trip, bring back a new sarong, the perfect at-home wear in warmer climes and something that should be in every Naughty Girl's bureau.

When Nicole goes to Europe, **she packs either all black with black or black with gray or combos of gray and charcoal.** She also packs black or gray boots and shoes and gray, silver or gold sandals. Her accessories: a gold or silver cuff, and one of two gigantic statement necklaces that she owns, both costume pieces. Her tote holds all her medications, jewelry and phone, and the rest of her wardrobe goes into one carry-on. She never checks in luggage if she can avoid it and once went to Europe for two weeks with only a carry-on and tote.

She gets a lot of use out of that tote. Hers is 16 by 17 inches with outside sleeve. It's easy to stash everything in and fits nicely under the seat. It houses what she might want easy access to while on the plane, including water, books, magazines, moisturizer, iPod or CD player, medicines and all personal items.

Phyllis is learning to edit her suitcases. Recently, she flew to New York for an overnight visit to join a client for a meeting with producers of a national news show. **She made the trip without checking in luggage,** a first for her. She wore jeans, a nice sweater and a jacket on the plane and

Nice Girl
in the air

Ellen, my cousin, wore a frumpy old velour track suit on a flight to New York for a publishing job interview. The potential employer flew her out Coach and put her up at an airport hotel for the final round of interviews. It was down to four candidates for the job as executive editor of several trade magazines. She was the last interview of the day, so she had time to check into her hotel and change.

The suited stiff who sat next to her on the connecting flight from O'Hare to JFK, gave her a disinterested once over, grunted at her and turned on his iPod.

It turned out he was flying in to interview Ellen and the other three candidates. She did not realize the coincidence until she arrived at the interview, all primped up and in her black Prada suit. **But like I am always saying, you never get a chance to change a first impression.** She did not get the job.

Laura's Nice Girl carry-on for a 3-month trip:

- Two jeans, one dressier than the other, black
- One dressier pant or stretch slack, black
- Two crop pants, one tan, one black
- Five light-weight T-shirt tops
- One long sleeve shirt to layer under T-shirts
- One good black sweater
- One long sleeve pullover sweater
- One lightweight windbreaker
- Two pajamas
- Two scarves to dress up outfits or keep warm
- One swimsuit (buy a cover up)
- Three pairs of underwear
- Five pairs of socks
- Three pairs of shoes: one flat for dress, one walking shoe and one sandal

the same jacket with nice pants, pumps and a different sweater to the meeting. Her carry-on included a dressy sweater for that night, extra tops and boots for the cold weather, as well as her beauty products and meds.

Destination packing

The Naughty Traveler may be guilty of over packing, but whether her trip is long or short, for business or pleasure, she will have the right clothes for the climate. I'm not just talking about the weather. Besides checking the temperature of her destination, she is savvy enough to take into account cultural nuances from place to place, especially if she is a business traveler.

A Muslim country is the obvious example. You leave your Naughty Girl short skirts, tank tops and spaghetti strap dresses behind.

In California, style is inspired by the red carpet. It's not so much about designer names, but how fabulous you look in the clothes.

East Coast fashion is designer conscious. You know the clothes you see in all the fashion magazines? In New York, they actually wear them. It's all about the Cat Walk and Wall Street. **The feeling there is not "look at me," but "look at what I am wearing."**

In Australia, which I often visit, you can wear shorts, dress shirts, flip-flops and go to the office. It's the most casual country I know.

Except for New York and Chicago, the U.S. is not a dressy country. Keep in mind, when traveling to other places, especially for business, that **in most European countries, it is considered rude not to dress well.**

I learned from my own mistakes a long time ago when I got off a plane in Germany and decided to take a stroll in a park along the Rhine without changing my clothes. I wore my True Religion jeans, my rubber Crocs and a T-shirt. **People were looking at me like I smelled bad and they didn't know my jeans cost $300.** That's when I started paying attention and saw that **the women were all in dresses and skirts with high heels for a leisurely stroll. The men wore sports coats or suits, even though it was Sunday and they were not at work.**

There is a thin line between dressing up and glitzing up.

Looking too flashy anywhere makes you a better target for pickpockets, so think twice about status handbags and diamond necklace. **Leave the expensive stuff behind. Don't take anything you couldn't bear to lose.** I know it goes against the Naughty Girl's nature to play it safe, but it's sometimes best not to stand out quite so much, depending where one is traveling.

Trashy Girl
in the air

A good look if you want to earn points in the Mile-High Club

With all the piercings these days, I often wonder how anyone makes it through the metal detectors at airports, and how do you explain some of them to the security personnel as they scan you?

Remember, when you sit in an airplane seat, short skirts really ride up. Unless you want to give cruising at 30,000 feet a whole new meaning, be careful. Although a little leg in First Class never hurt anyone.

Fear of flying

As a very frequent flyer, I understand the need for comfort and practicality in selecting your flight gear. **What you wear on the plane has to be something you can eat, sleep, sit, stand and walk long distances in.** Yet, whether I'm flying First Class or Cattle Car, I see saggy asses and sloppy outfits, and this will not do.

Business travelers have to be polished and "on" for whatever presentation awaits, so when flying, it's tempting to let things slide in favor of total pajama-like comfort. However, baggy sweatpants and T-shirts are not okay, ever.

Jill lets things go so she can be "on" when she reaches her destination. She shuttles back and forth to see family in Ohio, and for vacations to Europe. She likes to wear comfy capri pants and flip flops or some sort of sensible flat. For long, sleep-over flights, she goes for an old sorority sweatshirt and worn-out sweatpants with Ugg boots, very much like she dresses around her home and in the hood. She also favors sweater sets in case she gets cold on the plane. And to complete the look, she may even bring a fluffy pillow. For her next birthday, I have to get her a new travel case or computer bag. Hers are worn out and tattered. You know, like the dog was chewing on one of the corners. In a travel situation these containers become your accessory, like a purse.

Tip:

Most women I know travel with a cashmere shawl that doubles as a warm blanket onboard, comes in handy in hotel rooms and can double as a shawl and wrap at night.

Naughty Girl
in the air

The Naughty Girl wears a comfortable yet stylish outfit, maybe a pair of tights with a longer, loose T-shirt style cardigan layered over a cotton tank. When she sits she still shows a little leg, and yet it's covered up.

Leggings with a long tunic-type top and cozy cardigan, a pair of stretch jeans that is not tight in the crotch with a tank or white T-shirt, and a long, cozy cardigan with ballet flats that are easy to slip on and off in the security line, are all ways to go in comfort and style.

The Naughty Girl's hair and makeup will be done and she will wear a feminine perfume so that as she squeezes into her seat her scent will be yummy and attention getting.

Like all frequent flyers, my canny French friend has a traveling uniform. It's always good to go, and for her, as always, it's all about good accessories. Her carry-on and foldable tote are shipshape. The tote is for what she needs on the plane: a bottle of water, books and magazines, iPod or CD player and all personal items. Once she lands, it comes in handy for day excursions.

Nicole wears a long-sleeved Empire-shaped or A-line black cotton T-shirt dresses over a pair of black bicycle shorts, and sandals and an enormous statement necklace. When she's headed for colder climes, she will adapt her costume: black tights with a black long sleeve polo T-shirt, black sweater coat or black velvet coat, black patent leather ballet flats and a wide, low-slung black leather silver-studded belt worn between hips and waist.

Naughty Girl carry-on:

- ❤ Sunglasses, eyeglasses and contact lenses
- ❤ Travel-size nail kit
- ❤ Cosmetics and beauty products
- ❤ Jewelry not worn on plane
- ❤ First-aid kit
- ❤ Medications
- ❤ Beauty products and makeup bag
- ❤ Fold-up nylon "extra" bag with handles
- ❤ Kleenex
- ❤ Handiwipes
- ❤ Woolite pouches
- ❤ Plastic gallon-size zip-lock baggies (perfect for holding damp things and potentially leaking stuff like shampoo, facial cleanser, etc.)

Traveling in style

There is a difference between wearing an old, loose, velour track suit and a cute Lulu Lemon sports outfit or cotton knit pants with a nice top or comfortable leggings with a loosely layered tank, T-shirt and cotton cardigan. These all look much more put together and still just as comfortable. Add to that a cotton scarf for a sense of style and to keep your neck warm and protected from the ventilation system.

You never know who may be standing or sitting next to you. Strike up a conversation. What have you got to lose? The man you are looking for might be in the adjacent seat. Maybe he is just flying back from a medical convention thinking, Oh my, what a hottie is sitting next to me.

But be sure to look for a ring or ring tan line before you leap.

Makeup on the plane:

For the flight, I suggest minimal makeup so as not to smudge it while sleeping (or attempting to do so). Lots of moisturizer, mascara, and a little blush and lip gloss are all you need.

Tip:

Stick to water, and lots of it, because air travel dehydrates your entire body and makes your makeup look dry and lined if you have dry skin and even oilier if you don't.

Space Savers

What to bring on board:

Carry on a toothbrush and toothpaste, antibacterial hand wipes, eye drops and a small travel-sized container filled with my Collagenesis Twenty-Four Hour Wrinkle & Dryness Relief Balm. Reapply throughout the trip.

Tip:

After a long flight, sprinkle a little baby powder in your hair. It will make your hair fluffier, less greasy.

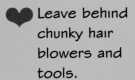 Leave behind chunky hair blowers and tools.

 Pack your 3-ounce portions of beauty products in your carry on.

Put single applications of shampoos, conditioners and lotions in snack-size zip-lock bags and label. When you are ready to use them, snip one corner with scissors.

9

Naughty at Church

Dressed in your Sunday best

My mother always wore her best for church and dressed us up as well to attend Saint Sophia Cathedral, the Los Angeles center of the Greek Orthodox community. She used to say that we are going to God's house, and we should look our best out of respect. That's the most convincing reason I can think of for making an effort to look great on Sunday.

The fashions women wear for religious gatherings depend, of course, on the age and location of the congregation as well as their religion. There are many churches, mosques, synagogues and temples where clothes must cover a woman's body, even her head, most certainly her arms.

However, in most houses of worship, this is not the case. **Generally, hats are a maybe, décolletage is a "no" and legs are a "yes."** And in some cases, all three are a go, especially for church parties and functions.

Are you single and looking to connect?

It pays to look your best when the man of your destiny may be seated behind you on Sunday or at the next church social. Church events and religious holidays are prime time for singles. At least that was the case where I grew up. The big event that brings single people together in the Greek Orthodox community is and always has been the Greek Folk Dance Festival, a four-day annual event every February. From pre-teens on, young people practice every week, and while the girls wear jeans to rehearsals, they always dress up in flirty, feminine dresses for the Sweepstakes Awards evening event.

Maybe it's the breath-taking beauty of Saint Sophia Cathedral that makes everyone want to dress up. They all put thought and care into their appearance. I've never seen anyone wear denims here. **On Sundays, the women wear diamond crosses with the latest fashionable dresses of all lengths or suits and always with high heels.** Their coiffures are lavish and their makeup perfect. Married or single, most of my Naughty Girl friends are actually more religious and go to their particular house of worship more often than most of the Nice Girls I know. Furthermore, they take great joy in presenting themselves to their very best advantage on Sunday and religious holidays. **And the higher their heels, the closer they feel to God.**

I asked my long-time Methodist friend Olivia what she wears to church in her home town of Nolensville, Tennessee, where she lives with her husband of 35 years, her childhood sweetheart James Haley.

When Olivia was crowned Ms. Senior America in 2008, it was after performing a rap song, "Don't Sit in My Pew." She adores being a star attraction and has a sense of humor about it and herself, especially among her friends at church who enjoy teasing her about her clothes.

For her, putting herself together is an artistic expression, and the people at her church get that and love her for it.

One day at church, the group leader passed out T-shirts with United Methodist Church written on it for the volunteers to wear at an upcoming event.

Olivia declined. "Oh, I don't do T-shirts with messages."

"If I had feathers and rhinestones, I suppose you might reconsider?" the leader asked.

Olivia shrugged and smiled. "I might."

Choir members can't wait to see what Olivia will wear to practice. **It will definitely not be jogging suits and running shoes.**

Often it's jeans, high-heeled cowboy boots, a T-shirt, long dangling earrings and necklace, and if it is chilly, a little shrug. She has gotten a lot of mileage out of the fox shrug she bought in Memphis.

She almost always wears high heels, even if she is walking around the farm in boots. She has good feet and lots of shoes. "I was raised poor," she told me. "My parents didn't have much, and I was lucky to have one pair of shoes. I remember getting a job and dreaming of being able to buy another pair." She doesn't leave the house unless she is photo ready and wearing eyeliner, lipstick, base and mascara. If she is rushed, she might skip the eyeshadow.

To be your Sunday best:

- Always make sure you look closely at your back in a full-length mirror before leaving home. People behind you are always looking at your back. No sleep-parted or flat back of hair!

- If you tend to perspire, avoid clothing that is too warm or restrictive.

- Don't drink soda or eat anything that makes you gaseous that morning. A stomach ache is no fun at church. People will wonder why you are perspiring.

- If you are single and looking, don't wear too much jewelry to church, especially rings. Men might assume that a boyfriend or husband is buying you this jewelry. Why risk it?

I have seen far younger girls I've worked with let themselves go a bit after a long day of appointments and presentations. But never Olivia. We worked together for years, and I can testify that with her Raquel Welch-style shag hair cut and trim body, she always looks super.

On Sundays she relishes putting together a special dress or outfit with unique jewelry. Olivia builds her wardrobe around black and white. She loves animal print tops.

Her favorite church outfit is a simple black pantsuit with a shell or tank top. She pins a big animal print or bright fabric flower that matches the top onto her jacket.

Or she might wear a flattering wrap dress by her favorite designer, Joseph Ribkoff. Last season it was a design with florals and zebra stripes, which she bought for Easter. Her accessories: a long necklace with onyx-like black stones and matching earrings and solid black patent heels with pointed toes and 3.5" heels.

They have five grandchildren now, but Olivia Haley is so not ready for the rocking chair yet. She is always on the go with commercials, print ads and videos as well as real estate.

"I don't dress my age. I'm not ready to go there. Age is just a number."

If that's not the Naughty Girl mantra, I don't know what is.

Nice Girl
meets the parents (or the children)

You say you are meeting his parents or his children for the first time after church services? You are all going out for pancakes together? **No matter how hot you are, this is a time to be a bit more conservative and let your Nice Girl show.** You don't want them to think you over the top or too sexy.

On the other hand, this is no excuse to look frumpy and bland. Nonetheless, here's where my Naughty Girl friends might pick up a few pointers from the Nice Girl. Like I said in the first chapter, **you always have to take into account the situation for which you are dressing.**

Regardless of age, you, Nice Girl, are what every mom and dad wants for their son. In fact, a Nice Girl is probably what your guy wants as well. **Likely it was the naughty that caught his attention, but the nice that won his love.**

If you are younger, the parents might see you as the provider of beautiful grandchildren and will be happy to see that you are attractive and healthy. So do wear a dress that flatters you shape without being too revealing.

If it's his little children you are meeting, they probably want to know that you will be a Nice Mommy who would be a good sport and love and care for them as well as their father, and not be a wicked stepmother. Don't wear anything that stains easily or impedes movement. **Wear something that shows you want to have fun.** Little ones love bright colors and clothes that make them smile.

If his children are older and no longer living at home, they also want to know you are not a gold digger who will eat up their inheritance. **Leave the blatantly expensive handbag, jewelry and clothes at home.**

While there is no reason to run out and buy something new, you still want to look attractive and polished. Anything that flatters your shape is the right ticket. **Soft and feminine is the safest way to go.**

Trashy Girl
at church wedding

What the invite should tell you:

♥ Daytime wedding: Get out your short dress or dressy suit. A soft floral dress or pastel suit is ideal. Forget sequins, black and glitzy jewelry if it's during the day.

No strapless, see-through, overtly sexy fashions for this affair. Hats and gloves are optional. Black is too funeral-like for daytime weddings, okay at night.

♥ Evening wedding: Cocktail dress. Discreetly sexy is good. You don't want to overdo the glitter or your makeup.

No, to anything sheer or too sexy, with skirts too short.

Yes, to dressy and glamorous, camera-ready for group shots.

♥ If it's a black-tie affair, that means long dressy or dressy short cocktail dress with bling.

♥ If it's a white-tie wedding, it calls for a long gown, and add even more bling, including furs.

Personally, I don't care. But somewhere it is written you should not wear white as a wedding guest because you're stealing the bride's thunder. It's an old rule, and so many women break it, especially in the summer for outdoor weddings. My friend Olivia, for instance, wears a long white eyelet dress and her turquoise jewelry. Proceed at your own risk. I can't be held responsible.

Naughty Girl
at Sunday services

Remember that often at church you have to impress the parents first and then meet the son or the older silver fox bachelor that might just be praying for someone just like you. **Sunday at church is the time to look feminine and soft** even if you are normally an edgy chick. Nonetheless, **try and be yourself and let your personality stand out as well.**

Rocket, an absolutely beautiful hairdresser I know on the West Coast, is an Angelina Jolie look-alike, only hotter. She always looks fantastic, wears heels and never goes anywhere without makeup.

She attends Catholic mass every Sunday and has several bright-colored, round-necked, above the knee, zip-up-the-back shift dresses.

She rarely wears pantsuits, but says they are fine for church, paired with a pretty blouse. "But only, of course, with high heels."

Beauty tips:

♥ Soft and feminine makeup is best for church. Stick to the concept of heavy eyes with light lips, or bright lips with soft eyes.

♥ Hot rollers make sexy, wavy, shiny hair for church. Men love to see hair that moves. It's sexy yet subtle. No one will think badly of you at church for having pretty, sexy soft hair.

♥ Taupe, gray, charcoal, plum and brown, are all great shadow choices for fall. In the spring, go brighter with your shadows in colors such as green, lavender, pinkish beige and blue. In the summer, be a bronze goddess and think browns, golds, coppers. Warm up your whole face with bronzers and a great fake tan.

♥ Catholic girls, beware of using too much sticky gloss, lest your hair gets stuck on your lips when you go up for communion.

Holy glow

Uncared for skin on arms, legs, neck and décolletage or shoulders is more obvious in the daytime. If you are going to a daytime wedding at church, make sure that exposed skin is especially soft, freshly scrubbed and moisturized. Try my Sweet and Smooth Body Scrub in the shower for an overall glow.

Sunday best classic makeup:

❤ Apply a light shade of shadow all over lid, then a darker complementary shade through crease and outer corner of eye.

Tip:

Try blending shadow with a powder brush dipped lightly in blush.

❤ Apply brown liner on outer corner of lower lid smudged towards inner corner and black liner on upper outer corner of lid smudged toward upper inner corner. Add lots of black mascara.

❤ Add soft blush, mauve or soft-toned creamy lipstick and just a dab of a non-sticky gloss.

Tip:

Church is not the place for fake lashes. Weddings and after-five church events are a different story.

Makeup for church is obviously different than makeup for a church day or evening wedding.

Yummy Mommy

Mom's the word

New mothers tell me that they feel sexier, more beautiful, more fulfilled than ever before.

Could that be the reason they project so much sex appeal, especially to their husbands and men in their lives?

What's that New Mom? You say you don't always feel that way?

Maybe you were the Naughty Girl who never thought she'd stop being foxy once motherhood came. And now you are wondering if you have time for a shower, let alone finding a new personal style.

The old style needs revision, that's for sure. **You could spread yourself too thin trying to maintain your glamorous ways.**

Yes, this book is about styling yourself to look sexy for all situations. However, I'm not here to lay a guilt trip on young mothers by telling them they should be pulled together all the time. For most mothers, when push comes to shove, baby always trumps grooming, and that's the way it should be.

"The first few months of motherhood are intense."

So says Meghann, a New Mom who inspired this chapter. "It's a constant round of diapers, sleepless nights, pediatrician appointments and dealing with getting out of the house with all the necessary baby gear needed. **It's the best of times and the worst of times.**

"The New Mom is waking up every few hours, her hormones are out of control, and she's trying to stay calm even though she feels like she has no idea what she is doing."

But then, Meghann says, after a few months go by, miracle of miracles, the New Mother is starting to think about going to the gym, pouring over fashion magazines and buying new clothes. Now, however, **she looks at clothes differently and is much more choosy and practical in her approach.** Many women find their figures have changed after birth and are dealing with weight issues. Some might revert back to the styles they wore in their youth or pre-baby days, when they felt more confident about their bodies. Others give up altogether and resort to sneakers and long T-shirts.

For New Moms, fashion is a delicate balance of looking good and feeling sexy.

Stylin' with Meghann

Before becoming an illustrator, Meghann designed costumes for theatrical productions, styled actors and actresses for their auditions and was a personal shopper. In short, she lives and breathes fashion. I got in touch with her a few months after her son Brogan was born. She was about to enjoy her first night out with her husband Ryan. She was wearing a new Cynthia Rowley royal blue flared halter dress and red platform wedges by BCBG.

"It's a big deal to arrange to leave my son, and I am really looking forward to this evening," she told me.

Every time I call, I tease her by asking what she is wearing and how she looks. She is always truthful, although at times it is painful.

"I'm not a woman anymore. I'm a Mom," she quipped once.

That was the morning that I caught her stopping for a quick coffee at Starbucks, during a walk with Brogan. She was wearing straight-legged cropped yoga pants, a baseball cap, an American Apparel V-neck shirt, no makeup and her hair in a ponytail.

"I think every New Mom knows that there are some days when you are completely on top of it, looking great, feeling good and ready to go.

Meghann's shopping tips for Moms:

When New Moms shop, they look at clothes differently. Instead of "Oh that's cute," several practical questions have to be answered. For instance:

- ❤ Can I bend over in this to pick up my son without showing the world my business?

- ❤ How can I breast feed in this dress without having to take it off?

- ❤ Could I carry my 20-pound son wearing these wedges without breaking my ankle?

- ❤ If I spill carrot baby food on this blouse, can I wash it easily?"

And there are other days when you are a hot mess.

"Most common scenario: I *have* to walk out the door in 10 minutes. I'm not dressed. My baby still needs to eat. It's not a debate. I leave the house looking wrecked, and my baby is clothed and fed."

Yet, she is learning to look forward to and value that time of day when she gets ready and often **makes a point of waking up before her baby just to have that moment.**

"It's my time when I can focus on me. When I have that time, I'm ready to conquer the day. I feel more with it. My time with my son is more present and inspired. **When I don't have that time, I feel a little more frazzled. I am in a constant state of catch-up."**

For New Moms, fashion is a delicate balance of looking good and feeling sexy, but also being comfortable enough to do what is needed without clothes getting in the way.

Achieving that balance will be easier once you reorganize your closet for your new life. If you are still dealing with weight issues, relegate pre-baby clothes that don't fit now, but might some time soon, to the back of the closet. Give away your maternity duds before you get too comfortable in them. And toss the pants that show your crack when you go to pick up your son. **Now put together two-to-three "Go To" great outfits for running out of the house.**

"I definitely have Nice Girl moments," says Meghann. "But there is a time when a New Mom begins to search for her own identity and figure out how she as an individual fits into her new life with a family."

How does she begin to establish more balance and sense of self? Part and parcel of that is finding a new style. "You can't run around in tracksuits and old jeans with T-shirts every day."

Tip from Meghann:

The Yummy Mommy is choosier as to what she wears and buys and doesn't settle. As a result, she is much happier with the fit and comfort as well as look of her clothes.

Nice Mom

With too much media attention on Moms who have it all and so much pressure for them to look good, it's no wonder New Mothers can feel torn in many directions.

The Nice Mom lives and breathes her kids, which is a good thing. She wears whatever is practical and functional to allow her to be as low maintenance as possible.

Just because you're a Mom, doesn't mean you have to wear jeans that say, "I'm not a woman anymore, I'm a Mom." The Nice Mom is prone to jeans with elastic waistbands, white sneakers, with turtlenecks, yoga pants and sweatpants. She often will wear her husband's sweatshirts or jeans because they are comfortable and easy to throw on.

Backless top—the
type that just
has ties keeping
it on

Tatoos all
over
her back

Pre-baby
jeans—way
too tight

Trashy Mom

Very high
platform
shoes

Naughty Mom

A male needn't be a Modigliani or Leonardo di Vinci to enjoy, celebrate and drool over a delicious, ripe, juicy Yummy Mommy.

The other day, I was lunching at the counter and noticed a table of three men who were watching a baby shower in progress at the same restaurant. The honoree, a tall, coltish brunette, entered with her baby after the others were seated. The young women all leaped up and gathered around her right in front of the men's table, cooing and giggling and oblivious to the male observers, who were transfixed.

I overheard one curvaceous lovely ask the honoree how she got back in shape so quickly. "I'm still struggling with my baby fat after eight months."

The New Mom looked fantastic in high heels and tight jeans and a V-neck fitted jersey that showed she had gotten her waistline back. The others wore short flippy skirts and T-shirts or jeans. They all had long, shiny hair, peachy skin and tan summer shoulders and arms.

Mommies' easy hair

I don't know why, but most Yummy Mommies have long hair. It's easier to keep. If you are lucky, it is wash and wear and you can run outside in the summer without using a blow dryer on it.

Yummy Mommy wardrobe basics:

❤ Everyday T-shirts in every variation. Long sleeved, short-sleeved and tanks, cotton and machine washable, in every color of the rainbow. Cheap is fine.

❤ Designer T-shirts for special occasions (James Perse, Theory), but not for finger-painting class with your little prodigy.

❤ Short flippy skirts

❤ Mid-length skirts

❤ Sundresses

❤ Jeans

❤ Yoga pants and tops

Makeup plan for Moms:

If your baby is so young, you don't have time for a full makeup: Simply brush bronzing powder all over face, including your eyelids, and add mascara and lip gloss or lipstick in your favorite shade.

When you have a little more time for yourself: Add my High Definition Mineral & Cotton Powder Foundation before you apply bronzing powder. Also apply eyeliner. This gives you a more finished look and will get you just about anywhere.

If you want to dress up things a bit, add one eyeshadow to complement your eye color:

Blue eyes—Light brown
Green eyes—Purple or plum family
Brown eyes—Rosy color

No Mom is going to wear more makeup until the kid's in high school.

Bibliography

Bayou, Bradley, *The Science of Sexy: Dress to Fit Your Unique Figure with the Style System that Works for Every Shape and Size*. Gotham books published by Penguin Group, 375 Hudson Street, New York, NY. Pub., 2007.

Brisben, Patty, *Pure Romance Between the Sheets: Find your best sexual self and enhance your intimate relationship*. Atria Books, a division of Simon & Schuster, Inc., 1230 Avenue of the Americas, New York, NY. Pub., 2008.

Demarais, Ann, Ph.D and White, Valerie, Ph.D., *First Impressions: What You Don't Know About How Others See You*. A Bantam Book, published by Bantam Dell, division of Random House, Inc. New York, NY. Pub., 2004.

Greenwald, Rachel, *Have Him at Hello: Confessions from 1,000 Guys About What Makes Them Fall in Love...or Never Call Back*. Previously published as Why He Didn't Call You Back. Three Rivers Press, imprint of the Crown Publishing group, division of Random House, Inc., New York, NY. Pub., 2009. www.crownpublishing.com

Hopkins, Christopher (the Makeover Guy), *Staging Your Comeback: A Complete Beauty Revival for Women Over 45*. Health Communications, Inc., Deerfield Beach, FL. Pub., 2008. www.hcibooks.com

In Style: Secrets of Style: The Complete Guide to Dressing Your Best Every Day. By the editors of In Style. Produced by Melcher Media for In Style Books and Time, Inc. Home Entertainment. Pub., 2003.

James, Dimitri, *Becoming Beauty*, Skinn Cosmetics Inc., www.skinn.com. 4733 Torrance Blvd. Ste. 974, Torrance, CA. Published by SSpreSS, a division of A Studio Z, Wimberly, TX. Pub., 2009.

Kearns, J. M., *Why Mr. Right Can't Find You: The Surprising Answers That Will Change Your Life—and His*. John Wiley & Sons, Canada, Ltd. 6045 Freemont Blvd., Ississauga, Ontario, L5R 4J3. Pub., 2007.

Krupp, Charla, *How Not to Look Old: Fast and Effortless Ways to Look 10 Years Younger, 10 Pounds Lighter, 10 Times Better*. Springboard Press, Hachette Book Group, 237 Park Avenue, New York, NY. Pub., 2008. www.HachetteBookGroupUSA.com

Lewis, Michelle Lia and Bryant, Andrew, *Flirting 101: How to Charm Your Way to Love, Friendship and Success*. Thomas Dunne Books, an imprint of St. Martin's Press. 175 Fifth Avenue, New York, NY. (first printed in Australia in 2003). www.stmartins.com

Nebens, Amy and Negrin, Jara, *Living the Posh Mom Life: The Fun, Fabulous and Fashionable Guide to Motherhood*, Sourcebooks Inc. Naperville, IL. *Guide to Motherhood*. Pub., 2007.

Oren, Leslie, *Fine, I'll Go Online! The Hollywood Publicist's Guide to Successful Internet Dating*. St. Martin's Griffin, New York, NY. Pub., 2007.

Patzer, Gordon L., Ph.D., *Looks. Why They Matter More Than You Ever Imagined*. American Management Association (AMACOM), 1601 Broadway, New York, NY. Pub., 2008. www.amacombooks.org

Pincott, Jena, *Do Gentlemen Really Prefer Blondes? Bodies, Behavior, and Brains—The Science Behind Sex, Love & Attraction*, a Delacorte Press Book, published by Bantam Dell, a division of Random House, Inc., New York, NY. Pub., 2008, 2005.

Rubin, Elycia & Mauceri, Rita, *Frumpy to Foxy in 15 Minutes Flat*: Fair Winds Press, Gloucester, MA. Pub., 2005.

Willdorf ,Nina, *City Chic: Modern Girl's Guide to Living Large on Less*. Sourcebooks, Inc., Naperville, IL. Pub., 2003. www.sourcebooks.com

Woodall, Trinny & Constantine, Susannah *What Not to Wear* by Riverhead books, New York, published by The Berkeley Publishing Group, a division of Penguin Group (USA) Inc., 375 Hudson Street, New York, NY. Pub., 2002.